Old Villita

Maury Maverick, Sr.

Mayor of San Antonio, Texas
Editor and Cooperating Sponsor

Compiled and written by the Writers' Project of the
Works Progress Administration, 1939

Reissued by Wings Press in celebration of the
Tricentennial Celebration of the founding
of San Antonio, Texas on May 5, 1718

and

La Villita Continues
by
Lynn Maverick Denzer

WingsPress

San Antonio, Texas
2018

Old Villita was originally published by the City of San Antonio as part of the AMERICAN GUIDE SERIES
Federal Works Agency / Work Projects Administration
F. C. Harrington, Commissioner • Florence Kerr, Assistant Commissioner • H.P. Drought, Texas State Administrator

Artwork in *Old Villita:* Original artists unknown.
Watercolors by Lynn Maverick Denzer. Used by permission of the artist.
Historical photographs MS 359: L-2317-H; MS 359: L-2357-A; and MS 359: L-2690-A
from the San Antonio Light archives of the University of Texas at San Antonio/
Institute of Texan Cultures. Used by permission.
Letters of Maury Maverick, Sr., from Dolph Briscoe Center for American History, University of Texas,
used by permission.
"In Old Villita" (music and lyrics) © 1940 by the City of San Antonio. Used by permission.

ISBN: 978-1-60940-528-1 (Paperback original)

E-books:
ePub: 978-1-60940-529-8
Mobipocket/Kindle: 978-1-60940-530-4
Library PDF: 978-1-60940-531-1

Wings Press
627 E. Guenther
San Antonio, Texas 78210
Phone/fax: (210) 271-7805
On-line catalogue and ordering:
www.wingspress.com

Wings Press books are distributed to the trade by
Independent Publishers Group • www.ipgbook.com

Cataloging In Publication:

Names: Maverick, Maury, 1895-1954, editor. | Denzer, Lynn Maverick, author. | Denzer, Lynn Maverick.
La Villita continues. | Federal Writers' Project. Texas, issuing body.
Title: Old Villita and La Villita Continues / Maury Maverick, Sr., Mayor of San Antonio, Texas, editor
and cooperating sponsor ; compiled and written by the Writers' Project of the Works Progress
Administration, 1939 ; La Villita continues / / by Lynn Maverick Denzer.
Other titles: La Villita continues
Description: San Antonio, Texas : Wings Press, 2018. | Originally published: Old Villita / compiled and
written by the Writers' Project of the Works Progress Administration, Maury Maverick, Mayor of San
Antonio, cooperating sponsor. San Antonio : City of San Antonio, 1939. | "Reissued by Wings Press in
celebration of the Tricentennial Celebration of the founding of San Antonio, Texas on May 5, 1718."
Identifiers: LCCN 2017041379 (print) | LCCN 2017051136 (ebook) | ISBN 9781609405298 (ePub
Ebook) | ISBN 9781609405304 (Mobipocket/Kindle) | ISBN 9781609405311 (Library PDF) | ISBN
9781609405281 (large format pbk. : alk. paper)
Subjects: LCSH: La Villita (San Antonio, Tex.) | Historic buildings--Texas--San Antonio.
Classification: LCC F394.S2 (ebook) | LCC F394.S2 F38 2018 (print) | DDC 976.4/351--dc23
LC record available at https://lccn.loc.gov/2017041379

Contents

Old Villita

La Villita Continues

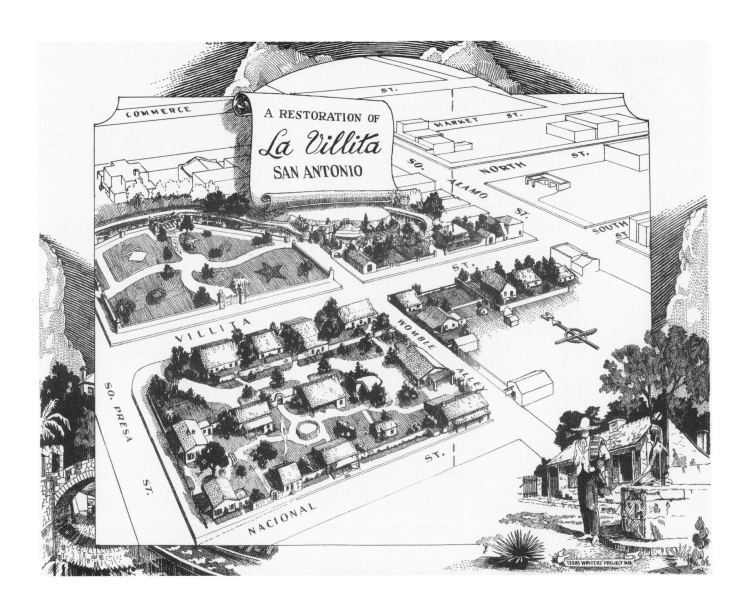

A RESTORATION OF
La Villita
SAN ANTONIO

Old Villita

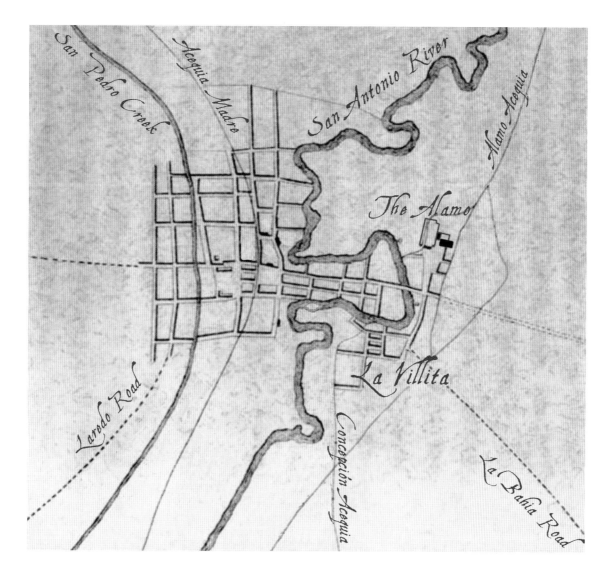

Adapted from a mid 19th century map showing San Antonio de Bexar as it was ca. 1836.

Introduction:
A Restored La Villita

In San Antonio, the restoration of *La Villita*, the "Little Town" of the Spaniards, has been begun as a historic and architectural monument. Few American cities have such an area, endowed with great age and a distinct and unusual character, partially intact and altogether adaptable to reconstruction.

It is planned, when restoration is completed, that a block-square area almost in the heart of the city's business district shall present an authentic picture of early-day San Antonio—the San Antonio of adobe houses with hand-carved mesquite doors; of flower-bordered *acequias*, ditches dug to supply water for the fields of Indians; of shady patios with feathery exotic plants, perfumed by rich blossoms trailing over high stone walls. The two centuries of La Villita's existence will echo here in windows with deep recesses, shake-shingled roofs, rough flagstone walks, worn stone doorsteps.

To save this storied district from inevitable destruction, the City of San Antonio, through Mayor Maury Maverick, in 1939 secured the area bounded by Villita, South Presa and Hessler Streets and Womble Alley.

Funds and facilities of the National Youth Administration were secured, and the initial work of clearing the site and of laying bare the ancient construction of the buildings was begun.

Seven houses were selected for restoration, but these will by no means complete the project, as plans have been made to add several buildings and features, so that, finally, a complete and authentic "Little Town" will be re-created.

The district demonstrates in its architectural features the expression of several types and generations of people. When disturbing later construction has been removed, these old houses will tell much of the architectural story of San Antonio and the Southwest—of the Spanish colonial, Texas colonial, European immigration, and several later epochs.

Of the section, O'Neil Ford, supervising architect representing the National Youth Administration, has this to say:

These houses are not of self-conscious architecture. They were built by men who were seeking a new and permanent security in a new land. The houses they built were elemental structures providing the minimum requirements of comfort and shelter.

Because confusion exists as to the precise date when the houses were built, it was decided not to attempt a restoration to definite years, but only to definite periods. Historians and architects have agreed that the restoration of the Little Town shall be from its earliest construction, about 1722, to include the 1850's, when the last radical changes, repairs, and redecoration occurred. New work will be consistent throughout with the period indicated by each building.

Of restoration methods, Mr. Ford says:

At no time do we expect to affect picturesqueness or "sweetness" at the expense of good sense or structural honesty, either in those things we may build or in the parts we may restore. The men and women of the historical societies are agreed that we will not make this a series of precious little surprises and features of interest, but that we will make every effort to have one general atmosphere of cool shady places, of profuse banks of blossoming native trees and shrubs ... surrounded by houses returned as nearly as possible to their first condition.

This plan bars all touches of theatrical and bizarre architecture, so easy to fall into in a work of this kind.

Painstaking attention to the authenticity of small details occupies the restorers of La Villita. Doors and mantels will be made in the workshops of the National Youth Administration by Mexican woodcarvers; a variety of window types will illustrate the form evolved locally; photographs are being made of details in other old houses scattered about San Antonio, and, from these, shop drawings are perfected as a guide to decoration, cabinet work, hardware, and even structural details. Plans call for the type of planting used by early-day Spanish residents in San Antonio, with native trees and shrubs, and even the walks will be of authentic materials.

The prime objective of this restoration program has been to produce, in La Villita's old setting, and on its old foundations, a carefully re-created group of small houses that show clearly what indigenous culture here evolved.

La Villita, restored, will be no museum of buildings, and no mere replica, but a living demonstration of how Southwestern architecture grew.

Tentative plans include the following features:

1. An encircling wall to insure privacy and such isolation as is necessary to create an atmosphere of the past.

2. Restored or reconstructed houses lining the outer borders of the area and having entrances both on the bordering streets and on a large inner court or plaza.

3. The addition of a large structure to be used as a restaurant of typical early-day Spanish colonial type, the cuisine to be Mexican, with service from the kitchens of the main building to vine arbors in the inner plaza.

4. A building to house a Hispanic-American library and museum, planned to be of adobe with the first floor some four or five feet below the ground level. The second floor, which would be used for meetings and social gatherings, as well as for the display of relics, would be reached by a wooden staircase through a balcony.

5. Along the south boundary of the area, a row of open stalls with stone or hewn wood shelves, where various Mexican arts and handicrafts will be displayed. Small workshop courts will be in the rear of each house.

6. The inner court or plaza, which will be beautified by careful planting, the judicious use of fountains, and a typical acequia. This plaza will be used for social events, and here diners will be served at tables under the stars, as were those who first sat at San Antonio's open-air chile stands in 1813.

While *dulce* vendors squat in the shadow of the little courts and *tamale* women swathed in *rebozos* scent the air with their pungent pots of steaming edibles, strolling *caballeros* wearing broad, braided *sombreros* and short jackets of green silk will sing to their own stringed accompaniment the songs of old Mexico and Spain—and the notes of the guitars, the odor of *masa* cooking, the soft voices of Latins, will help roll back the years to the time when these songs, these houses, these were San Antonio.

Part of the value of this restored La Villita—as seen by its patrons and sponsors—is historical. Part is architectural. And part is the charm and distinction it will present to visitor and native son alike.

—Maury Maverick
Mayor of San Antonio, Texas
1939

The Story of La Villita

We have no city, except, perhaps, New Orleans, that can vie, in point of the picturesque interest that attaches to old and antiquated foreignness, with San Antonio. Its jumble of races, costumes, languages and buildings; its religious ruins, holding to an antiquity, for us, indistinct enough to breed an unaccustomed solemnity; (all) ... combine with the heroic touches of its history to enliven and satisfy.

—Frederick Law Olmsted,
in *A Journey Through Texas*, 1837

Many others, like Olmsted, have been struck by the visible evidence of history in San Antonio; for here it is possible to *see* the past in old, scarred buildings. As the oldest remaining residential area of the city that has grown in dramatic stages beside the banks of the San Antonio River. La Villita—the "Little Town" of the Spaniards—has stood not on the fringe of events, but within their often stormy center. Villita has had the sometimes good, sometimes bad, fortune to be always a small but highly romantic part of the tale that has been woven beside the twisting river for more than two centuries.

First to dwell on the site, as far as recorded history shows, were the Coahuiltecans. These sedentary Indians had village sites along the river valley; their brush and hide tepees stood under great pecan trees. The women cultivated patches of beans and maize. Where La Villita is today, flint tools of these tribesmen are sometimes found, testifying to the primitive community that was the Little Town's forerunner. Ashes of long-dead fires, found many layers deep, often contain blood-red arrow points made of flint

Known picturesquely, according to Mrs. Esther Perez Carvajal's research, as "The House Where the Sun is Born."

quarried at some unknown distant mine and later shaped here. The great fear of these peaceable dwellers on the river bank was of cannibal Karankawas from the Texas coast—powerful, evil creatures who came up the stream in canoes, seeking plunder and man-meat.

Here, in the spring of 1536, came a stranger who was to write the first description of the area, Alvar Nuñez Cabeza de Vaca, a Spaniard who had survived the expedition of Panfilo de Narvaez. The red men who dwelt on the banks of the river received the Spaniard kindly. Dr. Carlos E. Castañeda, eminent Texas historian, says :

> They (the Spaniards) were ... given presents of ochre, beads, and a few little bags of silver....They were by this time in the vicinity of present day San Antonio, where the Indians had established a rancho because of the natural facilities of the region for settlement. "If this deduction of

mine is true," declares Or. (Robert) Hill, after many years of painstaking study, "then San Antonio is the oldest identifiable village within the present limits of the United States."

Since the site of La Villita is one of the most desirable in the San Antonio River Valley, it is reasonable to conclude that at least part of the rancho described later by Cabeza de Vaca was in this locality. Here the villagers would have been safe from the constant menace of river floods. If this assumption be true, then this is one of the oldest places of habitation to be described as such, in this country.

More than a hundred years elapsed before Don Domingo Teran de los Rios, breaking new trails for the King of Spain, halted at an Indian village on the banks of this river while Father Damian Massanet said Mass and named the valley, San Antonio. Other *conquistadores* passed this way, and in 1714 the Indian villagers were visited by the French explorer Louis Juchereau de St. Denis, who said it was a "likely spot for settlement."

The river that winds past modern Villita Street received its name in 1709 from a friar who never forgot the "richness of the grapes of all kinds, the quality of the mulberry trees which surpassed those of Murcia and Granada, the abundance of nuts, more tasty than those of Castile . . . and the large number of wild turkeys and deer, to say nothing of the herds of numberless buffalo." Father Fray Antonio de San Buenaventura Olivares had so great a desire to claim this area for God and King and to win the "more than fifty Indian tribes" of the San Antonio Valley that he began a campaign of persuasion which was to end in the establishment of the most famous of all Franciscan missions and its suburb, La Villita.

The "Little Town" is Born

On April 25, 1718, Don Martin de Alarcon, Knight of the Order of Santiago, "Captain General and Governor of the Province of Tejas and such other lands as might be conquered, entered the valley of the San Antonio with men and implements sufficient to found a settlement. The persistent dream of Father Olivares had resulted in this expedition, its tangible manifestations including 1,000 bleating sheep, 548 horses, 200 oxen and as many cows—and, vastly more important, 72 persons who were pledged to convert this wild and beautiful valley into a Spanish outpost of civilization. The friar who had brought all this to pass had quarreled with the dashing Alarcon, and marched in alone, barefooted and dauntless, to found—on May 1—Mission San Antonio de Valero, known today as the Alamo, shrine of Texas liberty, world renowned because of a battle in which every defender died.

Five days after the mission had been founded, Alarcon established the *Villa de Bejar* on a site near San Pedro Springs. Thus in the beginning, the civil settlement of present-day San Antonio was west of the mission, and the soldiers and settlers lived apart from the Franciscan outpost that was to rule their destiny. But in 1722, on orders of the Marquis of Aguayo, the *presidio* (fort) of the mission and the homes of the colonists were moved—because of the constant threat of Indian attack—to a spot near Mission San Antonio de Valero. In the archives of

San Francisco el Grande, headquarters of the Franciscan Order in the New World, is a document, the report of Father Olivares to the Viceroy, which says:

He (Alarcon) likewise succeeded in establishing a Spanish villa and presidio in the valley of San Antonio, with thirty families, in the most pleasant spot to be found in the entire province where (they) enjoy the greatest advantages and facilities anyone can desire.

Frederick C. Chabot, in *With the Makers of San Antonio,* has this to say of the Spaniards who were to become the founders of La Villita:

Alarcon ... was therefore instructed to establish a colony of Spaniards on the banks of the San Antonio, with at least thirty families or settlers, with soldiers, conceding to them in the name of His Majesty, all the favors and privileges accorded by the royal laws.... It was also ordered that the soldiers in Texas serve for the erection and construction of settlements. It was particularly ordered that at least ten soldiers be left for the defense of the mission ... on the

San Antonio River.... It was also ordered that the Spaniards and soldiers, who were to remain at the mission, were to be married and have their families with them as the Indians were surprised when the soldiers did not bring their wives.... Most noteworthy of all (in Alarcon's expedition) was the company of militia.

Chabot's list of the military men who were to create homes for themselves in La Villita include names old in modern San Antonio: "Don Diego de Escobar, and family; Alferez Francisco Hernandez, and family; ... Geronimo Carbajal, and family; Antonio Guerra; Don Francisco de Escobar; Domingo Flores, and family; Xtoval de la Garza; Sebastian Gonzales; Joseph Ximines; ... Don Francisco Juan de la Cruz, Master Mason; Santiago Peres, Carpenter; Joseph Menchaca," and many others whose descendants today are San Antonians.

Conflicting reports of those who actually participated in the founding of the Villa in the valley of the San Antonio obscure the actual number of soldiers and settlers who came to dwell among the Payaya and other tribes of Coahuiltecans. It is reasonably certain, however, that in 1722, when the *Villa de Bejar* was moved to the vicinity of the mission, which was somewhere in the neighborhood of modern Alamo Plaza, the first few huts of La Villita may have been erected. J. M. Rodriguez and other writers, telling the stories handed down in San Antonio's oldest Spanish families, claim that La Villita soon grew as a place of residence of the married soldiers of the mission garrison. Rodriguez in his *Memoirs of Early Texas* says:

Villita, meaning little town, was settled by some of the soldiers who came with the Mexican Army and those who had intermarried with Indians, and who were not supposed to be the very best people. In fact there was a great distinction between the east and west side of the river. The west side of the river was supposed to be the residence of the first families here, and the descendants of the Indians and Spanish soldiers settled on the east side of the river.

From legend and scattered fragments of early-day writings, the story of the presidio and the adjoining area which probably extended to the locality now known as La Villita can be pieced together. Robert Sturmberg in his *History of San Antonio and of the Early Days in Texas* (St. Joseph's Altar Society), wrote:

Viceroy Marquis de Valero, knowing the dangers that beset the newly founded Mission, ordered Martin de Alarcon ... to send a strong military protection to the Mission San Antonio de Valero. Thereupon, in fact during the same year, 30 soldiers with their families were moved ... to the new Mission site. A small village was built for them close to the Mission (on the east side of the river), and it received the name of San Jose de Alamo. In later years when the Missions were abandoned by the Franciscan Fathers, the soldiers moved into the Mission.... Of the Villita San Jose there is no historic information available to the writer with the exception that the huts or houses were located close to the Mission San Antonio de Valero.

That the modern Villita area must have been at least on the fringe of "Villita San Jose" is attested by old land records and other ancient documents in the archives of Bexar County. Among the petitions for land and deeds to property is one actually describing a typical house of that area:

Mathias de la Cerda sells to Joseph Salinas, a soldier of the presidio: A house of stone and mud, 12 varas long and five wide, with a jacal that serves as a kitchen all of woven twigs and grass ...

For this house and its grounds the soldier paid "four she mules ... thirty mares ... six gentle horses, give or take...."

Another typical house is described by a Mrs. H. Lucas, who wrote, of San Antonio in the 1850's:

This was a very primitive town when we first came here. The houses were one-story and built of adobe, one room deep with dirt floors, and no connecting doors leading from room to room; a person went outside to enter another room at the back. The sills were more than a foot high, the window sills were three feet wide and the walls were three feet thick. The windows were iron-barred and one could sit in the window seat and chat with a passerby or flirt with an admirer. The floors were of dirt and kept hard by sprinkling and sweeping with brooms of brushy wood tops.

Soon after the establishment of the mission, Indian neophytes and soldiers and settlers were given the task of digging one of San Antonio's several *acequias* (irrigation ditches). To water the fields of the Mission San Antonio de Valero—covering land now occupied by tall buildings in the heart of the city—the Alamo Madre Ditch was dug from its source near the head of the river (in the neighborhood of present-day Olmos Park), and one of its branches passed beside the east walls of the mission. William Corner in his *San Antonio de Bexar (A Guide and History),* wrote, "From here (the mission) it passes on through the Menger courtyard; thence to supply, in old times, the inhabitants of East Villita." Chabot, in *With the Makers of San Antonio,* wrote:

> They had worked four years in bringing water from the river to the fields. All the work had been done with bars, and the missionaries themselves had not lacked a single day of work. President Father Joseph Gonzales was especially zealous, and was the one who worked the most, for he appreciated the importance of irrigation to his mission.

The Alamo Madre *acequia,* lined with willows and figs, probably brought the first beauty to the narrow, rutted streets of La Villita. Harking back to those remote days of which there are so few chroniclers, Sidney Lanier, as quoted in Corner's *San Antonio de Bexar,* painted an imaginary picture of the people of that frontier community:

> Ah, here they come, the inhabitants of San Antonio, from the church-door; vespers is over; the big-thighed, bow-legged, horse riding Apache steps forth, slowly, for he is yet in a maze—the burning candles, the shrine, the genuflexions, the chants, are all yet whirling in his memory; the lazy soldier ... the soldier's wives, the squaws, the catechumens, the children, all wend their ways across the plaza. Here advances Brother Juan, bare-footed, in a gown of serge, with his knotted scourge a-dangle from his girdle; he accosts the Indian, he draws him on to talk of Manitou; his pale face grows intense and his forehead wrinkles as he spurs his brain on to the devising of arguments that will convince this wild soul before him of the fact of the God of Adam, of Peter, and Francis.

The Wrong Side of the River

Tradition says that during the next few years La Villita—linked inseparably to Mission San Antonio de Valero because it was the *villa* of its soldiers—was a poor little district of adobe huts, whose yards and gardens alone were pretentious. Difficulties beset the struggling, isolated Spanish outpost: shipments of food and clothing, of *pesos* due the soldiers, were few and disappointing when they did come. Yet the plight of the soldiers' families was not emphasized until the morning of March 9, 1731, when fifteen families from the Canary Islands marched in—and were promptly given the title of *Hidalgos,* "sons of noble lineage," by a grateful King who had long despaired of colonizing this wilderness with permanent settlers. The titled *isleños* (islanders) founded the royal *Villa of San Fernando* across the river from the Villa de Bexar, on present-day Main and Military Plazas. At once the newcomers adopted an attitude of isolation, closing their homes to the folk from the "wrong side of the river," thus inaugurating a class distinction that was to rankle for many years.

The Rev. Mother Louis (Morin) of the Ursuline Academy, on Navarro Street, is descended from the Curbellos—one of the original sixteen Canary Island families brought to San Antonio. She said (in 1939) that Señor Juan Curbello built his residence on property later known as Bowen's Island—where the 31-story Smith-Young Tower now stands—and that this district, close to Villita Street, was devoted to small "farms" or gardens where flowers and vegetables were raised. Mother Louis said:

> Villita was built for the soldiers and their wives: the Canary Islanders were considered noble people and the soldiers' families, common people; and the soldiers' quarters were thus in a different place from that given to the aristocratic Islanders of the San Fernando settlement.

Sturmberg, in his *History of San Antonio and of the Early Days in Texas,* wrote:

> In following this narrative it is well to bear in mind that the Mission San Antonio de Valero and the village San Jose de Alamo located on the east side of the river; and the city of San Fernando and the Presidio de Bexar, located on the west side of the river, constituted two different communities, each having their own civil administration. They even had trouble about their respective water rights for irrigation purposes.

San Fernando was the capital of the province of Texas, and its grandees led a gay, luxurious life as compared with the humble existence on the east side of the river. Gregorio Esparza told of the folk who lived in the *jacales:*

> We were of the poor people ... to be poor in that day meant to be very poor indeed—almost as poor as the Savior in His manger. We were not dissatisfied with it.... There was time to eat and sleep and look at growing plants. Of food we had not overmuch chile and beans, beans and chile.

Evil days fell upon the people of the San Antonio Valley, rich and poor alike, between 1731 and 1750. The Apaches, stirred to fury by the coming of more white men to their old hunting ground, made raid after raid upon the settlements of the King. Horses and burros were stolen from off the very streets of Bexar, and finally, on June 30, 1745, the warriors planned to burn the presidio and wipe out the twin Villas. A boy of the mission gave the alarm, and at once the soldiers and neophytes of San Antonio de Valero went into action. Castañeda, in *Our Catholic Heritage in Texas, 1519-1936,* Vol. III, describes the event:

> One hundred mission Indians came to the rescue and so stoutly did they attack the invaders that they were soon put to flight. The soldiers and Indians now gave chase.... The fate of Fort St. Louis (La Salle's fort in Texas) might have been the fate of San Antonio had it not been for the timely aid of the mission Indians of Valero ...

A quarrel caused by the policies of a new governor, Carlos Franquis de Lugo, soon developed between the religious authorities of the mission settlement and the civil heads of San Fernando. This controversy became serious when the governor ordered the mission guards removed. Growing ill feeling was climaxed in the autumn of 1736 when the padre in charge at the mission attempted to close the one small bridge over the river that connected the two Villas. It is recorded that the governor, who had heard that even he was barred from the narrow span, crossed the bridge in heated defiance,

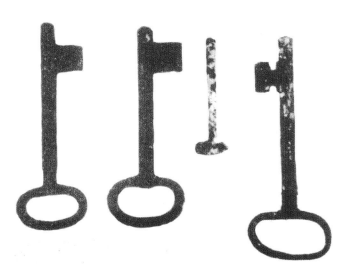

Hand wrought keys discovered under plaster.

faced the padre in his cell, and threatened to send the missionary back to Mexico "packed on a mule." Father Mariano de los Dolores, the rebellious priest, was forced to leave the bridge open, but retaliated by closing the church of the mission to San Fernando's faithful. Mission guards were not restored until 1737.

In 1762 Mission San Antonio de Valero was in its zenith. Those dependent upon its bounty drew from the resources of the mission rancho, described as having "one hundred and fifteen gentle horses, one thousand one hundred fifteen head of cattle, two thousand three hundred sheep and goats, two hundred mares, fifteen jennets and eighteen saddle mares." (From *Documentos para la Historia de la Provincia de Tejas*, pp. 163-167.)

In that year the walls of the chapel of the mission collapsed, a symbolic event, for the fortunes of the mission flock were never again to rise. The following year, 1763, a plague decimated the ranks of priests, neophytes, soldiers and settlers. Of this era Sturmberg wrote:

The decline of the Mission San Antonio de Valero proceeded very rapidly from 1763 on. The savage Indians preferred to follow the French doctrine—preferred the wild and easy life to the orderly life of the mission. The older, converted Indians and their children soon acquired the habits of the soldiers and their families; many of them moved out of the mission into the Villita San Jose de Alamo and

their children married with the children of the Mexican soldiers.

Indications are that by this time the region of La Villita was peopled not only by families attached to the mission, but by soldiers of the Presidio of Bexar, a royal garrison maintained for the protection of the Villa of San Fernando and the older mission settlement. In his diary Fray Gaspar de Solis, in 1767, tells only of soldiers attached to the Presidio. Yet the Villa of San Fernando still frowned upon La Villita as the home of less aristocratic Spaniards, the home, as Rodriguez says, of the families of soldiers. Solis, by the way, wrote a remarkable description of the San Antonio River in this area:

The road from the presidio is wooded with mesquite, huisaches, pin oaks and oaks. The river contains fish: barbos, piltontes, seafish, sardines, eels and others. In these woods ... are great numbers of cattle and horses, many animals such as deer, wolves, coyotes, rabbits, and now and then a lion, some wild cats, wild boar along the banks of the river, blue ducks, geese, turkey, ... screech owls which do not call like those outside, but have a different manner of screeching ...

The historian Bancroft tells of a 1778 law which dealt a telling blow to the mission and its dependents. The measure provided that all unbranded cattle were the property of the King of Spain, and imposed a fee of four *reales* a head for all such cattle slaughtered. Edward W. Heusinger in *Early Explorations and Mission Establishments in Texas* explains that, "Since the wealth of the missions consisted in cattle, which it was impossible to herd together and brand, this double-toothed law practically obliged them to pay four reales apiece for the right to slaughter their own cattle raised on their own lands."

Records disclose that in 1785 the two settlements of San Antonio—that on the east side of the river, including La Villita, and that on the west side, the Villa of San Fernando—became one civil unit under an alcalde—a sort of justice of the peace and mayor combined. Until this year, La Villita and all the mission settlement had been under the jurisdiction of the padres.

A movement was now under way for the abandonment of the missions and the secularization of their lands. The Count Revilla Gigedo in his report as Viceroy said, "Neither our acquisitions nor the number of Indians congregated in the actual mission towns do by any means justify the enormous outlay incurred, nor the fatiguing labors undergone by the missionary fathers." In 1790 there arrived in San Antonio refugees from the Presidio of los Adaes, in east Texas, and to these victims of French aggrandizement many of the lands formerly held by Mission San Antonio de Valero were distributed, including, as old land records disclose, lots in the present area of La Villita. By 1793 the mission beside the San Antonio River had been abandoned, and the families who had lived so near it, obedient to its bells, lost their separate identity and became at last simply citizens of Bexar, as this Spanish town was most commonly known.

Speaking of the San Antonio of 1793, Sturmberg wrote:

On the south side of our present-day Gas and Electric Company's plant where there are two bridges, there was located the principal ford for wagons and riders on horseback. For the convenience of the general public a log was thrown across the narrowest part of the stream.... Where Villita Street begins or ends on South Alamo Street, there was the main part of the Villita. After crossing the stream one entered at once into the city of San Fernando.... Houses were built closely together; they were all the one-story kind and topped with flat roofs. The construction was the only practical one for warding off the at-

tacks of savage Indians.... The combined population of the city and Villita never exceeded 2,000 or 3,000 souls, whilst at times, it fell below those numbers.... The peninsula, formed by the river and extending to the Alamo, was called Protero. There was also a collection of houses around the Mission San Antonio de Valero (the Alamo) and extending to the Villita.

And now the "Little Town," safe so long under the protection of the padres and their soldiers, was thrust out into the often turbulent life of the city beyond the river.

Stormy Times in Little Town

Forlorn and impoverished. La Villita drowsed on the river bank and remembered better days; and the faithful few who had been taught their *Aves* in the now deserted mission trudged with little relish to the Church of San Fernando across the river—the haughty, gold-trimmed church of the equally haughty, goldbraided *isleños*. Bells that had called them to vespers were silent now, and many an old man, ragged and barefoot, stood abashed in the new church of the Canary Islanders, heartsick for the friendly old mission chapel that had never known nor sought magnificence.

In 1803 the solitude of the abandoned Mission San Antonio de Valero was broken by the arrival of the Flying Company of San Carlos de Parras, which occupied the former living quarters of the monks. This military unit hailed from the Villa of San Jose y Santiago del Alamo in Mexico, and its claim to immortality was to bestow the name Alamo upon the battered old mission. Henceforth, records refer to San Antonio de Valero as "the Alamo." Chabot, in *With the Makers of San Antonio*, wrote: "Many of the soldiers of the Alamo Company married Indians and established their homes in the vicinity of the mission. Then Spaniards purchased the old mission lands, and gradually a new town grew up there, which was called *La Villita*." Thus, it is indicated that the period in which the Alamo received its famous name saw also the naming of the eastern part of the old settlement of the mission as "Little Town."

Meantime the germ of freedom had invaded even the isolated outpost of Bexar, and men of republican persuasion were whispering of revolt from royalist Spain. In 1811 a stirring episode took place among the soldiers of the San Antonio garrison, quartered then in La Villita. In his *Memoirs*, José Antonio Navarro tells how the spirit of revolt seized 2,000 troops of the royal guard holding Texas between San Antonio and the Sabine River. Navarro wrote:

> Stationed there were officers of the most famous troops of Nuevo Leon and Nuevo Santander.... San Antonio was at the apogee of its prosperity. Thousands upon thousands of gold and silver coins arrived in the city every two months for the luxurious maintenance of the troops. It was a very common occurrence to see any given soldier spend $100 for breakfast: and with the same serenity as we might now invite a friend to join us in a glass of beer.... Common to all human society the citizens and troops of San Antonio began to suffer some anxiety concerning the political fate of Mexico.... The descendants of the first Isleños, settlers of Bexar as legitimate original Hidalgoes, who were those with the greatest daring, suggested methods of humiliating the haughty Spanish governors.... Three sergeants were then chosen to seduce the army. They were Miguel Reyna, Blas José Perales and Trinidad Perez. These placed the entire troop on a war footing in the barracks, which at that time was in the place known as La Villita here in San Antonio. At dawn, January 22, 1811, they offered this army to the Captain of Militia of Nuevo Santander, Juan Baptista Casas, who accepted the honor and was placed in command of 1,500 men.

The revolting troops, led by Casas, marched to the "Plaza of the Government," and imprisoned the Spanish governor Salcedo, Herrera, and other Spanish officers who still slept in the deep slumber of the haze of early morning, confident that no one would dare to attempt anything against their omnipotent persons." Navarro added:

This memorable day of January 22, 1811, was the first on which the Mexicans of San Antonio de Bexar announced their desire to break forever the chains of their ancient colonial slavery.

Captain Casas sent his prisoners to Mexico; but the republican revolt had turned, and Casas was finally betrayed by his own compatriots, imprisoned and at last shot for treason. Thus a resident of La Villita, young and zealous, made the first of San Antonio's spectacular sacrifices for freedom. Others quickly followed; in 1813, the "Republican Army of the North," composed of Anglo-American adventurers, Mexican liberals, and Indians, occupied San Antonio, to be defeated in August, 1813, by the Spanish General Arredondo, whose vengeance against the revolutionists almost emptied La Villita of its men. In the barracks of the town nearly 800 prisoners were assembled, and most of these were shot. Inside a small, almost airtight granary 300 prisoners were retained overnight, and 18 suffocated. That night (August 20) is called *La Noche Triste* (the sad night) in San Antonio history. This was the time when the women of the town were confined in a building derisively called *La Quinta* (the household), and made to convert 24 bushels of corn every 24 hours into *tortillas* for the victorious royalist soldiers.

Spanish persecution of the families of liberals was so drastic that the residents of San Antonio, including those of La Villita, fled whenever opportunity for escape was presented. Since La Villita had given birth to the republican movement locally, it suffered most of all.

Echoes of the dark days of 1813 are found in the archives of Bexar County, in petitions of the remaining Bexar citizens for shelter, food, or for life itself. There is the plea of Luisa de Luna, for example, who said in a petition to the *Cabildo*, or city council:

> That being one of the most unhappy women in this province because my husband Vicente Travieso was one of those carried away by his caprices and want of judgment to help the iniquitous party of the insurrection for which reason they have sequestered everything that belonged to my husband and me.... And all this has

been taken from me as well as my personal clothing and so I have been reduced to misery and want, I and four small children … So I apply to the benignity and powerful protection of your highness in order that, moved by pity you will have the charity to give me one of the rooms of the house known as mine, one of the small cows so that my unhappy and unfortunate children will have something to nourish them ….

This petition ended with the words, *No se firmar*—"I cannot sign." The plea, made on November 22, 1813, was granted that same day when the district commissioner, Don Alvino Pacheco was ordered to give the unfortunate woman "the house which was seized from the traitor Francisco Ferias."

Many of such petitions in the archives name boundaries of property within the present Villita area. Land granted by Spanish authorities was still occupied by means of primitive gestures of possession: the grantee pulled weeds, broke branches from trees, scattered handfuls of dirt about, drove stakes, and otherwise indicated the process of taking possession of the land.

A Cloudburst Brings Aristocracy

La Villita had been born of piety and nurtured through bloody episodes by its simple faith in the traditions it was heir to from a scarred old mission. Yet if was a humble place, a cluster of primitive houses huddled close for security and reassurance. Its people were humble folk for the most part—largely a mixture of Indian and Spanish blood. Its fortunes, always linked—even though intangibly—with the mission, had reached perhaps their lowest ebb when a natural disaster intervened to change the entire complexion of the area.

In July, 1819, a flood deluged the proud Villa of San Fernando, causing considerable loss of life and carrying away buildings and the houses of grandees. The waters of the San Antonio River and of San Pedro Creek overflowed every part of the city except the higher ground of the Alamo and La Villita. Governor Martinez reported that "On the morning; of the 5th instant, in consequence of a terrific waterspout (doubtless what now would be called a

House redecorated by Middle-European immigrants, on Villita Street.

cloudburst) which burst north of the city, the river became so swollen as to run over its banks, causing a general overflow such as has never been beheld in the province before."

Martinez said that the damage was such that "the city may be said to exist no longer," and that its inhabitants, "those who were not victims of the fury of the waters," were reduced to "lamentable destitution." The governor added, "The landed estate belonging to the Royal Domain has been ruined by the overflow." Chabot wrote of the events that followed:

> Subsequent to this flood began the migration to La Villita … where the Martinez family received several royal grants…. What today is known as the Cos house, on Villita Street … was, according to the abstract of the property, a grant to Don Antonio Martinez.

The Bexar County archives have many petitions of the period from the hidalgos of San Fernando who wished to move to Villita's higher ground. Such a petition is the following:

Donicio Martinez, a citizen of San Fernando, prays for a tract of public land in the new Villita, as the site for a house which he desires to occupy as a dwelling.

Old as was Villita in that day, it is to be noted from this application that, to those of the upper class who now thought it desirable as a dwelling; it was "new" Villita.

Thus, from the time of the 1819 flood, began the change of Villita from a lowly community of modest homes to an exclusive residential area where lived many of the oldest and most aristocratic families of San Antonio. This character it was to retain for many years. Not all the former land owners in La Villita wished to sell at once, but the inducement of profitable prices for small lots that had been granted them by the King gradually had its effect. For awhile Villita presented the contrast offered by fine and humble houses in proximity. As Mrs. Lucas wrote, "The back yard or patio was either a place with a fountain and flowers or it was just a dust heap with a scraggly cactus in a corner and a skinny rooster in search of insects in the dust pile." (From *Memoirs of Mrs. H. Lucas, Frontier Times* Vol. 3, Jan., 1926).

The Scene of Surrender

On the streets of San Antonio, as the nineteenth century entered its second decade, *Americanos* in increasing numbers appeared. Although this old town was still Latin, the influx of colonists brought by Anglo-American *empresarios* (colonizers) to widely scattered communities in the now Mexican province of Texas (for Mexico had won its independence in 1821), had naturally increased the non-Latin population.

Among the newer residents was Erastus (Deaf) Smith. He had come to Texas in 1819, and wooed a belle of the town, half French and half Spanish, whose parents lived in La Villita. When the couple was wed in 1828 they at once established their domicile in the house which still stands at 301 South Presa Street. Deaf Smith had earned a reputation for courage among the Indians and Spaniards; his name was to become well known in Texas history, and soon, for again the idea of freedom was gnawing at the minds of many who walked the streets of the old pueblo. Throughout the province, those newly adopted *Americanos* spoke and dreamed of a day when this land might be wrested from Mexico.

During these years La Villita again knew the scourge of Indian warfare, as indeed did every person dwelling in the San Antonio Valley. The *Menchaca Memoirs* (Chabot) tell how the prices of food rose, because, "by reason of the city being surrounded by Indians, the people (were) unable to get out of town." A sack of corn sold for $5, a pound of coffee was $2.50, and tobacco was $1 an ounce. "The people being in such pressure, would at the risk of their lives go out in the country to kill deer, turkey, etc., and cook herbs for the support of their families," Menchaca wrote. "The persons who were engaged in agriculture had to go in squads of fifteen or twenty or more to look for their oxen; and while working had to keep their arms with them." Menchaca described the murder of one Domingo Bustillos by a Tonkawa, placing the scene near La Villita.

Into this atmosphere of unrest and trouble, in 1828, came a handsome brown-haired, blue-eyed stranger—James Bowie, onetime slave runner for the pirate Lafitte, a chivalrous adventurer known—although some credit the invention to his brother Rezin—as the creator of the bowie knife. Bowie met and became enamored of Ursula Veramendi, Spanish beauty of San Antonio, and many were the silks and satins and velvets aired along Villita Street when the dashing frontiersman and the aristocratic beauty were married in San Fernando Church on April 22, 1831. And there were tears in Little Town, when, in 1833, the news came that Bowie's lovely wife and their babies had died in Mexico of a plague. That tragedy almost broke the heart of the man whom Texas Indians had given the name Fighting Devil, and he no longer danced with the belles or teased the duennas of La Villita on occasions when the Spanish aristocracy made merry in the midst of growing anxiety. For the talk of freedom had now become a war; in 1835 a motley army led by Stephen Austin, first Anglo-American colonizer and known as the Father of Texas, upon San Antonio and encamped along the river near the Old Mill, at a site occupied today by a residence at 1215 North St. Mary's Street.

Bowie had returned, but this time as an enemy, and his old friends kept their relationship a secret. For the town was held by a Mexican general, Martin Perfecto de Cos young and handsome, but not the man to brook alliances with a rebel Texan.

The Little Town was under the direct scrutiny of the Mexican general, for according to tradition and certain writers, he occupied the adobe house at 513 Villita Street—a small building that remains today as it was then, low, long and narrow, with few windows and thick walls. In *The Rise of the Lone Star*, by Driggs and King, a San Antonio pioneer is quoted thus:

General Cos lived while in this town in a little adobe building which still stands on Villita Street. Father saw and talked to him there. The General conversed freely and seemed to bear no animosity....

The Texas colonial revolutionists arrived near the city in October, 1833, and had several skirmishes with Cos' troops, but never near Villita. Then on December 4, when the officers had decided to abandon the siege, and their soldiers—cold, hungry, ragged and unpaid—had started breaking camp, a bold frontiersman named Benjamin F. Milam shouted, "Who'll go with old Ben Milam into San Antonio?"

The answer of those Texas volunteers—farmers, tradesmen, lawyers, adventurers—is outstanding in Texas history. They followed "old Ben Milam" into San Antonio, and after five days of fighting, in which Milam was killed, they took the city. And now a historic scene occurred in the little house on Villita Street.

General Cos was a brother-in-law of Antonio Lopez de Santa Anna, dictator-president of Mexico, and Cos had been sent to Texas to subdue the rebels. In this he had failed. On December 9, he flew a white flag from the Alamo, where at first his guns had boomed defiance and warning to the Texans, and under a flag of truce made a verbal offer of surrender; then withdrew that part of his army which was in the center of the city to the Alamo side of the river. On the cold morning of December 11, in the little building that is now at 513 Villita Street, he faced the Texan commander, Gen. Edward Burleson, to discuss articles of capitulation.

Here those terms of surrender, providing for the withdrawal of the Mexican army from Texas, were written and signed. One condition stressed by Burleson was that a large group of convicts, who had been brought in chains to San Antonio as reinforcements for Cos, must be all taken by the general himself to below the Rio Grande. Brief excerpts from the historic document signed on Villita Street follow:

Capitulation entered into by Gen. Martin Perfecto de Cos, of the Mexican troops, and Gen. Edward Burleson, of the colonial troops of Texas.... Being desirous of preventing the further effusion of blood and the ravages of civil war, we have agreed upon the following stipulations: First. That General Cos and his officers retire with their arms and private property into the interior of the republic under parole of honor that they will not in any way oppose the re-establishment of the federal constitution of 1824. Second. That the 100 infantry lately arrived with the convicts, the battalion of Morelos, and the cavalry, retire with the general, taking their arms and 10 rounds of cartridges for their muskets. Third. That the general take the convicts brought in by General Ugartechea beyond the Rio Grande.

On December 14, at dusk, General Cos led his vanquished troops from the Alamo and Villita areas. Whooping, jubilant Texans swarmed into the Alamo, and the houses of La Villita must have been shuttered and dark, for the Little Town knew not these tall, noisy strangers with their buckskin garb and long squirrel guns.

The Cos House, where San Antonio was surrendered
to the Texans on December 9, 1835.

When the Alamo Fell

But as days passed many of the Texas soldiers remained—although many drifted homeward, confident that the revolution had successfully ended—the eastern bank of the river learned many agreeable things about these newcomers: even shared, in several instances, the enthusiasm of the volunteers for freedom from the tyrannical rule of Santa Anna. Some of the homes of La Villita now even gave of their men to this cause, for the old families had always had a weakness for revolutions.

In Ehrenberg's *With Milam and Fannin*, a soldier who was fighting for the unrecognized Texas rebel government told of the days that followed Cos' departure:

> The restoration of peace had brought back to the city many of its residents who had deserted it during the siege. With the return of the fugitives, bustle and animation again filled the streets, where Texans and Mexicans walked about their business without fear or resentment. As we strolled in the main thoroughfares, we were pleasantly struck by the graceful gait of the attractive ladies, whose beauty brought back thoughts of the pretty New York girls I had seen up and down Broadway.... Mexicans are great pleasure seekers and spend their lives in dancing, riding, drinking, eating and sleeping. As we were welcome guests among many of the native families of the city, we visited them often.... Everybody looked contented: the men chatted with

the olive-hued beauties or talked of horses. Besides conversation, cracking pecan nuts or smoking cigarettes seemed to be the most absorbing pastime of the whole assembly.

Meantime in Mexico Santa Anna prepared an army of more than 6,000 men to crush the Texas revolution. Gen. Sam Houston, former governor of Tennessee and now a leader in the Texas cause, sent Bowie to destroy the Alamo so that it would not fall into Mexican hands; but the little garrison that remained was unwilling to evacuate the post. If the Mexican army could be held here, they argued, the settlements of the Austin Colony and others might escape destruction. So, in the winter of 1835-36, the tall señores continued to frequent the streets of La Villita. Among them was Col. William Barret Travis, red-haired lawyer known as the "gallant captain" who shared with Bowie the military responsibility, and David Crockett, the famous Tennessee backwoods congressman who had recently said to his late constituents, following his defeat for reelection: "You can all go to hell—I'm going to Texas."

The closeness of La Villita to the Alamo linked the hardships of the Texas soldiers and the uneasiness and privation of the families of La Villita. Food, clothing and money were scarce for both; San Antonio had been cut off by the revolution from its ordinary sources of supply and commerce. As the long winter days passed, rumors of an invading Mexican army made occasional ripples in the deep pool of common hardship and hunger. As spring approached, Mexicans of the town who were in sympathy with the issue of freedom for which the Texans fought, including the father of J. M. Rodriguez, warned the soldiers of the Alamo that an army—now known to have cost Santa Anna $7,900,000 in its preparation—was being prepared below the Rio Grande to reconquer the rebellious province. Amelia Williams, in her thesis entitled *A Critical Study of the Siege of the Alamo and of the Personnel of its Defenders* (manuscript, University of Texas), wrote that: "Finally Travis told him (Rodriguez) that he and his men had to stay and die at the Alamo, if need be, fighting for Texas."

Rumor became certainty on the morning of February 23, 1836. Before dawn of that day an atmosphere of excitement spread from the humble *jacales* of the poorer Mexican district west of San Pedro Creek. Ox carts lumbered through the rutted, twisting streets, piled high with the household goods of departing San Antonio Mexicans. Travis, pricking up his ears, demanded the reason for this exodus, but most of the hurried travelers were loyal republicans and made evasive answers. As chickens squawked and pigs squealed while their owners carted them away, and cows lowed and children shouted, the Texas leaders stood in the midst of the confusion and realized that the invading army from below the Rio Grande must not only have started, but that its arrival must immediately impend.

Travis placed a sentinel in the bell tower of San Fernando Church, to watch for signs of an approaching enemy. At noon he reported figures with glittering lances moving in the direction of Alazan Creek. Scouts sent out encountered the vanguard of Mexican cavalry. The bell of the parish church rang out the alarm, and soon the soldiers of the Alamo were at their posts. Between 185 and 200 men comprised the garrison, and there were 18 small guns along the fortifications. Each of the volunteers had proved by remaining here that he was indeed determined to "die if need be."

In the flurry that followed news of the rapid approach of the Mexicans, Davy Crockett said calmly to Travis, "And here am I, Colonel; assign me to some place, and I and my Tennessee boys I will defend it all right." Miss Williams wrote that "Travis then replied that he wished Crockett to defend the picket wall extending from the end of the barracks on the south side to the corner of the church." That order was to become most important to La Villita, for Crockett's cannon, during the twelve days of the siege, sent its projectiles into that section, and much damage—although it is unrecorded—must have been done.

By two o'clock in the afternoon of that first day Santa Anna's forces had occupied the town. A blood-red flag, the flag of no quarter, flew from the tower of the church of San Fernando. Santa Anna's demand for unconditional surrender was answered by the Texans with a cannon shot fired from their eighteen pounder—Crockett's gun. The siege of the Alamo had begun.

What followed is a story known to all the world, the story of not more than 200 men facing fully 5,000 picked troops in an uneven struggle that was in its effects to end in the independence of Texas.

For the tattered soldiers inside the Alamo there were days of cannonading and a few encounters of a minor nature as hope of reinforcements dwindled and finally died. James Butler Bonham, boyhood chum of Travis, had borrowed money to come to Texas and fight beside his friend; he tried in vain to bring relief to the beleaguered garrison. And although the houses of La Villita were deserted, since all women and children had abandoned the city for safer places, much of this historic struggle occurred in and near the Villita area. Proof that at least one of the Mexican batteries was here is contained in a letter from Travis to the president of the Texas convention, then in session to declare independence from Mexico:

Commandancy of the Alamo, Bexar, March 3, 1836.

To the President of the Convention, Sir: ... I beg leave of you to communicate to you the situation of this garrison.... From ... the twenty-fifth (of February) to the present date the enemy have kept up a bombardment from two howitzers ... and a heavy cannonade from two long nine-pounders, mounted on a battery on the opposite side of the river.... During this period the enemy have been busily employed in encircling us with entrenched encampments on all sides, at the following distances, to-wit: In Bexar, four hundred yards west: in Lavillita, three hundred yards south.... Their threats have no influence on me or my men, but to make all fight with desperation and that high-souled courage that characterizes the patriot, who is willing to die in defence of his country's liberty and his own honor.... God and Texas—Victory or Death.

Mrs. S. J. Wright, in *Our Living Alamo*, has also mentioned the Villita battery. Old reports and maps show that the branch of the Alamo Madre acequia that passed beside the Alamo's east walls, now known as the "Villita ditch," separated the besieged Texans and the besieging Mexicans on the east side of the mission fort. General Cos, forced by Santa Anna to break the parole given by him after the Battle of San Antonio, was assigned to attack the southeast fortification (including the chapel of the Alamo, the only building in the fort that remains today), and his command was stationed near La Villita when at last orders were given for an attack on the Alamo.

Mexican batteries were silenced by ten o'clock of the night of March 5, as preparations were made in profoundest silence by the Mexicans for a daybreak assault. That night, Little Town must have known the quiet creeping figures of dragoons as they went quietly through the darkness, collecting scaling ladders, crowbars and axes to use in the attack. These soldiers were obedient to the dictator yet fully conscious of the bloody dawn but a few hours distant. None knew better than these hired fighters of Mexico the awful price they would have to pay for the Alamo, for they had sampled the aim of the long rifles, and had tested the endurance and courage of the tall señores.

A Mexican soldier writing to his brother said, in a letter published in *El Mosquito Mexicano*, April 15, 1836:

> I marched under the immediate command of General Cos, and I will tell you what I saw. After a long wait we took our places at 3 o'clock a.m. on the south side, a distance of 500 feet from the fort of the enemy. Here we remained on our stomachs until 5:30 (whew! it was cold), when the signal of march was given by the President from the battery between the north and east.

Thus, part of the attacking forces were in the direction of La Villita. At the rise of the moon Mexican troops completely surrounded the Alamo; within, its defenders slept, for this was their first respite in many days from constant cannonading. Sentinels had been posted but they must also have slept, for they gave no alarm. Coffee might have kept them awake; they had no coffee.

At five o'clock on the morning of March 6 Santa Anna stood upon the Commerce Street bridge, whose approach is on the spot then occupied by a Mexican battery. To the wild notes of the *deguello*, a bugle call that for centuries had been associated with "no quarter," the legions of Santa Anna moved forward to awaken the ragged handful of Texans to their last dawn.

Of the battle thus begun on a bleak March day, of the hand-to-hand fighting, the desperate resistance, the death of every male defender inmate of the Alamo, much has been written. Blood ran that day in the old acequia that had watered the flowers of La Villita in happier times. Flames of the funeral pyre erected at Santa Anna's command—where the bodies of the Texas patriots were reduced to ashes—afforded ghastly illumination in La Villita that night. Only a few remained there to remember that horror; and for months afterwards, while all living people shunned the Alamo and its environs as a place of death, the homes of Little Town stood deserted.

The direct result of the Battle of the Alamo was the Battle of San Jacinto, where the independence of Texas was secured by the defeat of Santa Anna and his army. Deaf Smith, who had distinguished himself as a scout for the Texas army, in this battle won further renown by destroying Vince's Bridge—thereby impeding the advance of Mexican reinforcements, and preventing the escape of Mexican soldiers during the battle. Thus, a resident of La Villita helped avenge the butchery of the Alamo and materially assisted in the conquest of Santa Anna, its author.

Although today removed from the Alamo by modern streets lined with modern buildings, La Villita retains its inheritance as a part—however small—of the epic story of that shrine. Its narrow streets and venerable houses recall the days when Travis, Bowie, Bonham and Crockett were here. Grantland Rice, writing for the *New York Tribune* in 1916, said that they sometimes come back:

> There's a tramp of a ghost on the low winds tonight.
> An echo that drifts like a dream on its way;
> There's the blur of the spectre that leaves for the fight,
> Grave-risen at last from a long vanished day;
> There's the shout and the call of grim soul unto soul,
> As they rise one by one, out of death's shadowed glen,
> To follow the bugle - the drum's muffled roll.
> Where the ghosts of the Alamo gather again.

Newcomers to Little Town

While Texas pursued its career as an independent nation in the late 1830's and early 1840's, new faces were seen in La Villita, and again its history and character gradually changed. The land west of San Antonio was still unpeopled and dangerous, and the old city of the Dons was considered a remote and unsafe outpost—threatened by Indians, as in the past, but also, now by avenging expeditions of Mexicans. Yet more and more non-Latin settlers were becoming citizens. In 1838 the picturesque John Coffee Hays, called "Captain Jack," a mighty Indian fighter whose father had owned The Hermitage in Tennessee, came to San Antonio with a company of Texas Rangers, of which historic band he was the first duly appointed captain. In the *Memoirs of Mary A. Maverick, San Antonio's First American Woman*, a footnote on page 28 locates the domicile of Jack Hays within the Villita area:

Some buildings and the original fence of Hays' San Antonio home still stand on the N. W. corner of Presa and Nueva sts.

Hays was the most daring and skilful type of frontiersman, grammatical, gallant and well bred; time after time he saved Texas settlements from destruction at the hands of the fierce Comanches. Single-handed he once killed an entire advance scout of picked Comanche warriors. The hero of hundreds of battles, he was later to become San Francisco's first sheriff.

The Mavericks, Samuel A. and Mary A., came to San Antonio in 1838, and Mrs. Maverick became a valuable chronicler of her times. She told how Hays and two companions attended a formal ball given by the Yturri family for Mirabeau Buonoparte Lamar, President of the Republic of Texas:

(They) had but one dress coat between them, and they agreed to use the coat and dance in turn. The two not dancing would stand at the hall door watching the happy one who was enjoying his turn—and they reminded him when it was time for him to step out of that coat. Great fun was it watching them.

Mrs. Maverick described bathing in the river, which since earliest recorded history here had been a favorite pastime. Floating bath houses were beginning to appear in the stream; and following the afternoon bath at four o'clock a lunch was often spread; as Mrs. Maverick wrote, "we had a grand good time, swimming and laughing, and making all the noise we pleased." Scenes such as this were occurring where the river hugged Villita Street—where once the Indian wards of the Alamo had bathed.

With the 1840's came an entirely new element to La Villita—German immigrants imported by the society of nobles of which Count Solms-Braunfels, founder of New Braunfels and other Texas German settlements, was a leader. A number of these strangers in San Antonio were attracted to the Villita area because of its elevation above the river, and because the dwindling fortunes of many of the old Spanish families were compelling them to sell their holdings here. Others, crowded now by a growing town, wished to move where there were fewer neighbors.

A number of the aged houses of La Villita were crumbling, some were in ruins. Over the walls of some of these new plaster and mortar was placed by the neat Germans; new roofs went on, steep-pitched like those of the Fatherland. Thus a number of the buildings in this area assumed a Teutonic character, quaint and attractive, and prim little gardens replaced the opulence and tropic abandon of the old patios. Others of the old houses remained untouched, for their owners stayed on, a little resentful of the changes wrought by newcomers.

Among these innovations were matters of custom. In mid-afternoons the rich odor of coffee floated over the housetops, as flaxen-haired housewives had *Kaffee klatsch* with their neighbors.

Miss Julia Vogt, 505 Sixth Street, remembered how her family observed this genial custom:

We gathered between three and four o'clock in the afternoon, friends and neighbors would come in. They served coffee and cake, bread and butter, ham and cheese, and sometimes other things.

Miss Vogt also recalled that some of the Villita families who had chickens often had to gather eggs "all over Alamo Plaza which was all in brush."

Mrs. Anna Guerguin, 108 City Street, also a descendant of former residents of the Villita area, said that her family had five meals a day: Breakfast, then coffee or broth at ten a.m.; then dinner, coffee at four, and last of all supper." She also recalled that when birthdays occurred, friends went uninvited to participate in a feast and merrymaking. "As their friends had come to their birthdays and were welcome, so they in turn went to their friends' birthdays knowing that they would also be welcome."

A time-honored dish among these pioneer families is a salad made of boiled smoked herrings, beets, hard-boiled eggs, pickles, apples, Irish potatoes and dressing. This concoction was a standby in the new racial parts of La Villita. So also was *Gefeullteskraut*, a veal pocket stuffed with kraut.

And now Christmas in Little Town had a dual personality. The families of Spanish descent still trooped to worship in the church of San Fernando: still placed burning candles in their windows in the week before the birth-date of the Christ Child, to direct the wandering souls of Mary and Joseph to their abodes. Sometimes bands of performers in *Los Pastores,* a play of the Nativity, performed here

for their patrons. The San Antonio version of this Christmas drama, one of more than seventy existing in America, originated in the humble *jacales* of the trans-San Pedro area; sometimes the players had sponsors among wealthy old Spanish families.

So on Christmas Eve, from the patio of one of those old Spanish homes in La Villita one might have heard the five thousand lines of rhymed and unrhymed dialogue and song of *Los Pastores,* and from the house next door the merry sounds of a Middle-European celebration of Saint Nicholas. From one household, the shepherds of the play reciting softly as they knelt before the rustic manger:

Ah, the beauty of the Child.
With a mouth of coral.
It is my wish to cover thee
With the weaving of my love.

From the household nearby, the booming voice of a jolly Saint Nick clad in a red suit and with bushy white whiskers, as he distributed toys amid the uproarious enthusiasm of little and big celebrators.

Mrs. Albert Steves of San Antonio recalled a typical Christmas of the immigrants of those early days here, and particularly the delicious little cakes made with honey and anise seed which were baked in November in anticipation of the holidays. Although one local store—Pentenreider's—had toys for sale, many of the toys were made at home. Every household had a Christmas tree, and home-made ornaments included chains of glazed paper. Walnuts and pecans were gilded and hung from the tree by strings; but big red apples were the brightest and costliest decorations. The real celebration of the holiday occurred on Christmas Eve; it was inaugurated by a huge turkey dinner, followed by two ceremonies of present giving—one at the Christmas tree for the children, the other in a separate room for the grownups. The children of the household invariably gathered around the dinner table and sang *Holy Night.* On Christmas Day families exchanged gay, informal calls, and were served cookies and wines.

Yet though this new racial element, with its inherited love of music, art and drama, brought new life and the promise of a different type of achievement to La Villita, this area and indeed the entire city remained predominately Spanish—it was still a frontier outpost. Julia Nott Waugh in *Castro-ville and Henry Castro* quotes the diary of Auguste Fretelliere, who wrote:

The city of San Antonio at that time (1844) had about 1,000 inhabitants, nine-tenths of whom were Mexicans, and the Spanish language was generally spoken.... The [street] which is now Commerce Street bore the name of *El Potrero*. On it were about twenty Mexican houses, that is to say buildings of rock and adobe with flat roofs of mortar and gravel. They were one-storied and had usually only one door, and two windows with iron grills. A man might think himself in Palestine. These were the best houses. The others were *jacales* made of mesquite sticks more or less chinked with clay, with roofs of *tules*, a kind of rush that grew very abundantly in the San Pedro.

It is safe to assume that at least part of the houses of La Villita answered to one or the other of these two descriptions, and that they were in sharp contrast with the increasing number of residences of German families. Many of these immigrants, such as the Bardenwerpers, were of noble descent, and their homes were rapidly becoming centers of musical and dramatic efforts. Mrs. Sarah Eagar, who is credited with having been the first non-Latin girl born in San Antonio, moved in 1846 with her parents, the Wilson Riddles, to a house on South Alamo Street. Mrs. Eagar in 1959—active and in possession of all her faculties at the age of 97—said that the boundaries of La Villita were then considered to be from Villita to Martinez Streets and from South Alamo to South Presa Streets. The Riddle place, however, was decidedly on the outskirts of the smaller, older area near the river. Mrs. Riddle, who was from Virginia, found living conditions in San Antonio primitive and asked her husband, "Why did you bring me to this country?" To which he replied, "To see if you could stand it."

Wilson Riddle had been one of the victims of the several Mexican invasions against San Antonio in the 1840's, before he moved to the peaceful rustic environs of La Villita. He died only one year after he had become a resident of Little Town, of the results of a harsh imprisonment in Mexico.

To Villita in 1847 a new kind of figure came,

Rough plaster over native stone, with a tin roof of a later period.

a threadbare, earnest young minister, John Wesley DeVilbiss. He found "five or six ladies in the city (San Antonio) representing nearly as many churches—a Catholic, Presbyterian, Baptist, Methodist, and Episcopalian, and some others friendly to the gospel." The Reverend Mr. DeVilbiss attacked the practice of holding cock fights on the main plazas on Sunday mornings while he was preaching and was rescued from a "ducking in the river" at the hands of the town's gamblers by the warnings of the above-mentioned ladies. This Methodist parson and his colleague in San Antonio, the Rev. John McCullough, a Presbyterian, were hard pressed for quarters to house their infinitesimal flocks. The two Protestant preachers held services jointly; but DeVilbiss had his own Sunday School class, of which a member was Augusta Evans, the writer, who lived for a time in La Villita. Soon after this, DeVilbiss "took the preliminary steps toward building a church in the city." He told this story in *Reminiscences of a Superannuated Preacher* in the book entitled *Life of John Wesley DeVilbiss:*

I secured an eligible lot on Valita (sic) Street, and we elected five trustees ... I left San Antonio ... and ... visited New Orleans, Cincinnati, Pittsburg, Wheeling, Lexington, and Frankfort, Ky., and various other places. I did not get much money, but obtained a great deal of material for building, together with many things I knew would sell in San Antonio. Among other things, I obtained a good bell in Cincinnati, the price of which was $110. When I returned, I paid for our lot in hardware that I brought on, and felt that we were succeeding. We still worshipped at the courthouse on the main plaza. I made a frame upon which to hang our bell, and placed it on our Church lot. I wanted to let the people see that we had made a start. Our bell was on one aide of the river and our worship about a quarter of a mile from it on the other. I was sexton as well as preacher, and would ring my bell and then go over to meet my congregation. The Mexicans gave me the very significant cognomen of "El padrecito que time la campaña," "the little priest who owns the bell."

But Protestantism in the form of a church building was not yet to invade La Villita—Roman Catholic by ancient inheritance. The Reverend Mr. DeVilbiss sadly tells us that he never built the church for the bell; he was persuaded by Mr. McCullough to assist in building an adobe church "on Main Street ... with the understanding that we should occupy the house conjointly, and when we built they would return the material (furnished by DeVilbiss) either in kind or in money. Our bell was moved over to the new church.... This was near the close of the year 1847. About this time I learned that the title to our

Two types of construction, old and new, on Hessler Street.

church lot was not good, and we lost the lot, and did not receive even indemnity for the purchase money. This was a severe stroke to me, as I had felt that with the lot we had at least a good foothold on the soil of San Antonio; but now after two years' hard labor, we had no place to call our own."

A Decade of Change

The environs of La Villita were described in 1849 by John Meusebach in the manuscript collection entitled *Wurzbach's Memoirs and Meusebach Papers:*

There was a long row of 'dobie, flat roofed buildings running from where the Post Office now is to the Grand Opera House, from there close to the Alamo Church and grass and pear (prickly pear cactus) growing on the top of the houses; all along the bank of the river there were Mexican huts covered with grass. What is now Commerce Street was a lake of water with two rows of cotton wood trees as far as the Alamo Ditch. There were but few houses on the east side of the river. What is now West Commerce Street was very narrow and all small houses, the most of them flat and grass roofs and pear hanging into the street; the two plazas were surrounded by the same kind of houses.

Still other racial elements—notably Polish and French—came to La Villita in the 1850's and 1860's. Erasmus Andrew Florian was of the former group: a political exile from Warsaw, he came to San Antonio to help found one of the city's first banks. The Florians moved to La Villita when it was considered San Antonio's most aristocratic section, according to Miss Mamie Florian, 826 North St. Mary's Street. "I still pronounce the name of this district 'Veeheeta', which early residents called it." Miss Florian said in 1959. "Our old home is just across the street from the present Villita Art Gallery. La Villita was the home of the elite in San Antonio." Miss Florian said that one of their neighbors was Augusta Evans.

In 1858 the German citizens—including those of the Villita area—formed the Casino Association, a select social organization, and erected a club and opera house on Market Street (part of the old building is today occupied by the San Antonio Water Company). This center of social and cultural life was at the back door of La Villita, just across the river. These residents also founded, in this year, the German-English School, whose old rock build-

European immigrants added narrow porches.

ings—all intact—are occupied today by the San Antonio Junior College. This school at the present 419 South Alamo Street served the little boys and girls of La Villita for many years: in it they learned both German and English, and the girls learned to sew, paint china, and make wax flowers. Julius Berends, promoter of the school, was a former nobleman. He arranged for the first school building to be dedicated to the poet, Friedrich von Schiller. Terms lasted eleven months of the year. Some of the boy students rode horseback to school and gave riding exhibitions between classes.

In *The Alamo City*, Pearson Newcomb thus described La Villita during the 1850's:

> Alamo Street continued south from Commerce Street along the river to La Villita, a village consisting largely of thatched roof dwellings, relics of the mission building period.... La Villita, the little village or residence section established in the mission building period on the south bank of the river, still retains some of its quaint semi-ancient buildings.

Yet, though many of its houses were still unchanged, the Little Town must have showed unmistakable signs of transition. Dozens of families whose forebears came directly to San Antonio from France, Poland or Germany now occupied the old Spanish buildings, and had infused their particular types of plants, trees, architectural ornamentation, and customs into the area. Architectural changes especially became manifest, as Miss Florian testifies:

> In the early 1860's the little settlement of La Villita was considered an aristocratic residential section. Houses were scarce in San Antonio then: when my parents bought ours in La Villita, it was made of stone, and had only four rooms. My family added a room on each side, and there was a kitchen and servant's room in the yard.

The Florian residence at 510 Villita Street is an example of the sturdy type of architecture chosen by those who remodeled the old houses. Stone was the commonest building material, as it was cheap and durable; the builder was in each case the architect and designed or remodeled his house according to his needs.

Progress and Personalities

Across the street from the Florians lived the Diaz family, and here Rafael Diaz (who became a Metropolitan Grand Opera tenor) spent his boyhood. At that time the Florian place reached back to Hessler Street: then, as today, Womble Alley ran through from north to south, crossing Nacional Street.

The Lutheran Church of St. John, known to early residents of Villita as the Rooster Church because of the rooster on its weather vane, was already drawing its congregations to Nueva Street when the Florians became residents. The Florian children on

Sunday mornings watched the members file inside, the women each holding a prayer book across which a freshly laundered white handkerchief was folded. Residents of the Villita section were hospitable, Miss Florian remembers, doing much leisurely visiting.

Where the Public Service Company building is on the corner of Villita and South Presa Streets, for a time lived the family of Dr. Clifford in a house that Miss Florian said, "stood up high from the ground as if it were on stilts."

Mrs. Mary Elmendorf, 220 Arciniega Street, also remembers much of La Villita during the 1860's. Her grandmother, Mrs. Louisa Wueste, lived in the building occupied in 1939 by the Villita Art Gallery, 511 Villita Street. This housewife was an artist whose paintings adorn many San Antonio homes—all of the portraits cameo-clear, vibrant with feeling and color. On the northwest corner of South Presa and Nueva streets lived the artist Iwonski, a friend of Mrs. Wueste. Iwonski had come with the European colonial rush to Texas, had fought Indians, and milked cows. He was an exile from his country and eventually returned.

Mrs. Elmendorf remembers another one-time occupant of the house at the corner of Villita and South Presa Streets. His name was Lemnitzer, and he was a cabinet-maker, a wood carver and "a fixer"—"he fixed anything that needed mending." Lemnitzer compounded a salve which was used by many of the residents of La Villita; but though the salve is only an odorous memory, many of Lemnitzer's hand-carved wooden candlesticks and other articles of household use remain as prized possessions among descendants of his former patrons.

An enterprise that later became a large factory started on Villita Street, where Gustave Duerler inaugurated a candy manufactory. Mrs. Elmendorf said:

> Behind the Duerler home was a little adobe one-room house which faced Hessler Alley, as Hessler Street was called then. This little humble place was where the later Duerler candy manufacturing company had its sure beginnings. It can be said that candy was one of the products of old Villita; when a child I used to stand and watch them making it—pink candy, and white.

On the corner of Nueva and Presa Streets, Mrs. Elmendorf recalled, was the little grocery store of the Teutonic Mr. Kresser; the groceryman's wife was French, and when politics changed in Europe relations in the family were sometimes strained, "for Mrs. Kresser never forgot she was a Frenchwoman." Mr. Kresser built some small stone houses which he rented as apartments; these buildings were in a yard which had a well that served all the "apartment" dwellers.

Next door to the Kresser property on Presa Street, stood a one-story adobe building called "the haunted house." Children so feared this place that many of them refused to pass it, even while on their way to the little grocery to buy candy.

At the southwest corner of Villita Street and Womble Alley in those days lived a shoemaker named Scheuermann. He made high shoes of a sturdy build, and for years shod most of the pupils of the German-English School.

One of the residents of Villita Street was a fortune teller, Mrs. Geissler who lived in a small adobe house near the shoemaker. The lovelorn, the hard-pressed, the bereaved, all found their way to the tight-shut doors of the mystic.

On the south corner of Villita and South Alamo Streets was the McAllister residence, a one-story house. This was a musical center; a daughter married Professor Katzenherger, who promoted, directed and participated in lively, hearty home-talent "operas." A neighbor in the Villita area, a Mr. Lapentz, sponsored amateur dramatic events, especially featuring plays of Schiller and Goethe. Much of the early local effort toward development of music and the drama originated with one or the other of these. Daughters of the families of the district starred in theatricals held in the Casino, and were applauded mightily.

In the McAllister home the powerful soprano of the Professor's wife, Anna, was frequently heard practicing roles in *Martha, The Bohemian Girl* and other operas. Here the amateur perform-

ers were drilled and trained, with five of the six McAllister children taking part in each performance. So successful were the presentations that the oldest son, Willie, organized one of the city's first orchestras; the second son, Joe, a violinist, later became an orchestra leader, A daughter, Lula, became the first supervisor of music in the city's public schools.

Mrs. F. W. McAllister, 123 Slocum Place, had this to say of those old days in La Villita:

Looking back upon the residents of La Villita in the middle of the nineteenth century, one realizes the contribution made by the old countries to Texas. Considering this block-wide and three-blocks-long area of San Antonio, bounded

La Villita, "Little Town," seen in 1939 from an upper floor of the Smith-Young Tower.

on the west by South Presa, on the east by South Alamo, extending northward to the river and southward to Martinez Street, one is amazed by the number of interesting, cultured residents in that very small district.

A descendant of one of the French families of La Villita, Miss Biencourt, still lives on Villita Street in a residence next to the Art Gallery. Her great-grandparents were named Desmazieres and lived in a two-story stone house in the Villita area; orchards of peaches. pomegranates, persimmons and grapes surrounded the house, and the grounds were green and cool. In this home, in 1861, a dinner was given for Robert E. Lee and other Virginians. Mrs. Sarah Eagar, then a pretty young lady home from boarding school in Mississippi, tells that someone proposed a toast, mentioning a threatening war. She said that Lee lifted his glass and answered. "If Virginia secedes I go with her."

Many Villita families had slaves, yet some of them were Unionists. Conflicting emotions shook the Little Town during the Civil War, but the fighting was distant, and life continued here much as usual except that most of the men were absent.

Times Change . . . Villita Does Not

Following the Civil War, La Villita settled down to a placid and undisturbed existence. Modernity came slowly but surely to the other San Antonio streets of the Dons, but not so surely to Villita. Joined to the city now by law, by geography, and by extended settlement surrounding it, the Little Town nevertheless remained a close, closed community: its families in many respects lived as villagers of a section distinct from the remainder of the municipality. Old names were perpetuated, old customs continued, and although progress entered the venerable doors in the form of the individual achievement of its residents, La Villita presented an almost unchanged face to the world.

A storm in 1868 damaged some of the aged Spanish buildings. At eight o'clock of the night of May 19 a terrific pounding of hailstones began, and when it had finished roofs were torn, walls scarred and in some places broken, chimneys were crushed and windows smashed. Repairs entailed some redecoration.

La Villita was joined to the city beyond by bridges made of planks laid on barrels that floated on the water. White canvas bath houses also floated on barrels; bathing in the river was an increasingly popular pastime.

Charles Herff, member of a pioneer San Antonio family, recalled that when a cholera epidemic descended upon San Antonio at the conclusion of the Civil War, a new activity occupied the small boys of La Villita—as indeed it involved all the youngsters of the city. The municipal recorder announced that for every two rat tails delivered to the then city hall, called the "Bat Cave", he would pay five cents. The ancient nether regions of the houses of La Villita had a thorough exploration by small businessmen searching out rats.

Mr. Herff added:

Smallpox was prevalent every winter but we did not fear it. On the corner of South Alamo and Villita Streets stands an old two-story stone building and formerly there were two stone one-story buildings adjoining. These buildings were a hotbed of smallpox. Along these buildings on South Alamo Street ran a flagstone walk. School children were told to use this sidewalk and to by no means fail to spit on it. This was considered a preventative. We firmly believed this.

In the 1870's the families of La Villita were leaders in many developments of a cultural character. Prof. L. J. Schuetze, 520 Hays Street, recalled the old Saengerfests and Volkfests of this decade, large gatherings in San Antonio of German singing societies from all parts of Texas. Parades opened the conventions, and displays of fireworks, pageants, concerts and contests occupied the entire community for several days. These celebrations were usually climaxed on Bowen's Island, near La Villita, with mammoth picnics. Noted actors were presented at the Casino Club, and at Turner Hall amateur and professional vied for honors in many a melodrama.

In 1872 Sidney Lanier fraternized with the artistically inclined old families of La Villita, participating in local *Maennerchor* musical events. Lanier composed *Field Larks and Blackbirds*, a score for wind instruments, while in this atmosphere of hearty and enthusiastic musical endeavor.

Professor Schuetze spoke of the environs of La Villita in the 1870's and 1880's, revealing that many of the families living close to the river in the Villita and adjoining areas had ducks and geese, and these fowls congregated on Alamo Plaza at an iron fountain erected to furnish water for horses and mules. The Professor said:

> When I was a child I was afraid to pass that corner of Alamo Plaza, for the many ducks and geese were a real menace to youngsters, whom they invariably chased.

During the wild period from 1870 to 1890, when San Antonio was a wide-open town enriched by drives of longhorns to northern markets over the celebrated cattle trails, La Villita looked sedately on from its perch across the river: it had no part in the lurid night life and frequently fatal gunfights. In the gay 1890's its sons and daughters attended the "magnificent balls" and other social events of the lavish decade, but the ornate gingerbread architecture so cherished then did not invade Villita. A few of the old families moved to more spacious, less crowded sections, but their old houses were little changed, sometimes not at all.

And so the twentieth century arrived, bringing skyscrapers and paved streets; the paving was welcomed by Villita, which had long waded through mud or walked over ruts in the narrow thoroughfares. But the skyscrapers stopped just short of the old village.

Today, surrounded by the noise and bustle of a modern city, La Villita faces its greatest transformation—its restoration to the heydays of yesterday. Through its forlorn recent years, when the section stood forgotten and largely in disrepair, various civic-minded groups have urged its complete restoration. That the section has endured is due largely to the loyalty of its families, many of whom cling to their faithful old houses of stone and adobe. Since the acquisition of the block-square area by the City of San Antonio, its shabby little streets have been invaded by engineers, architects, artists, historians, city fathers, pioneers—all interested in or actually engaged in the project of restoration. Neglected so long, La Villita still seems a little aloof to all this interest and to-do.

The little village of the *padre's* day is being born again. To its creaking old homes youth is returning. When the present plans have been fulfilled, there will be patios again, with palms and poinsettias; there will be the tang of *tamales* in the air, the soft sound of *tortillas* being patted out by copper-colored women on *metates*, the plaintive notes of guitars accompanying such wistful melodies as *La Golondrina*.

The San Antonio of the distant past will he presented here, and on historic ground. Strife and turmoil may grip the outside world, but not this rejuvenated village of two centuries. Perhaps its future visitors may sense in it an unchangeable serenity, the seclusion and poise of time itself.

Opening Day
Celebration at La Villita
1941~

Above: Painting from a photograph of opening day at La Villita, with the statue of Father Miguel Hidalgo. The statue was a gift to the city by the President of Mexico, Manuel Avila Camacho, on behalf of the Mexican people.

At Left: Rosita's Bridge, at the Arneson River Theater. The bridge was named in honor of Rosita Fernandez, a much beloved local singer.

Below: La Villita Galleries and the Plaza Nacional.

At Left: "La Villita Shadows."

Below: Fiesta 1954, at "Night in Old San Antonio" (NIOSA), showing Terrellita Maverick as the snake charmer.

At right: The bell tower adjacent to Bolívar Hall.

Lynn Maverick Denzer 2016 ©

Above: Bust of Maury Maverick, Sr., in Maverick Plaza at La Villita.

Preceding page, at left: The Arneson River Theater

Preceding page, at right: Día de los muertos, outside the Little Church of La Villita.

La Villita Continues

Lynn Maverick Denzer

La Villita did indeed continue. Maury Maverick, Sr.'s *Old Villita* was written in 1938. This addendum—a short but eventful history—brings the story up to 2018, the Tricentnnial year of the founding of San Antonio.

I grew up hearing stories about La Villita from my grandmother Terrell, Maury Maverick, Sr.'s widow, and my mother Terrellita, his daughter. Their stories seemed to me and to others worth sharing. Those family tales, along with my own memories and additional research, will help me to tell the rest of the story.

Connecting History

In 1900, at the turn of the last century, five railways serviced San Antonio, bringing people and commerce to what was then the largest city in Texas, with a population of 54,000. Three major railway stations were located on the eastern, southern and western ends of downtown, with a fourth further south, close to the stockyards on Laredo Street. Thus La Villita, though still at the very center of downtown, was something of an island—detached from the surrounding business of the city, yet with a life of its own, important to progress.

St. Philip's Normal and Industrial School was founded in 1892, at what is now 502 Villita Street, as a school for young black women. The primary subject was sewing. In 1902, Artemisia Bowden, a pioneering African American educator, was hired as a principal/teacher. Under her direction, St. Philip's expanded into a high school—known as "Bowden's School"—and later a junior college. In 1917 the school moved from La Villita to its present campus on the eastside.

In 1910 there began an influx of Mexican immigrants to the city, almost all political exiles and refugees from the Mexican Revolution. Some settled in La Villita with their families. During the teens and '20s, alongside people living in their homes, several businesses began operating in La Villita, including Joykist Candy, Texas Ice Company, Dechman Coffee and Spice Mills, New York Star Cleaning and Dye Works, and The Texas Eagle Publishing Company.

The Riverwalk Approaches

From 1913 to 1921 there were six floods that plagued San Antonio. On September 9, 1921, all of downtown was submerged by as much as twelve feet of water. St. Mary's Catholic Church, built by Irish immigrants in the 1850s, partially collapsed into the river. Yet, the sturdy little village survived, mostly intact.

The river had been replaced by artesian wells as the primary water source for the growing city in the 1890s, resulting in the river periodically going completely dry. This, combined with the dangers posed by severe flooding, prompted proposals to drain the riverbend, turn it into a storm tunnel and construct the street over it.

The San Antonio Conservation Society, organized in 1924 by Rena Maverick Green and Emily Edwards, did not support the demolition of the river, and had other visions for downtown. That year they had entertained the City Commissioners, while selling their cause of river enhancement, by taking them on a river boat ride and later, at City Hall, presenting a puppet show, "The Goose With the Golden Eggs," penned by Edwards. The marionette puppet stars were the goose with golden eggs and the City Commissioners, themselves. The theme revolved around whether San Antonio's character and charm should be pushed aside to achieve prosperity quickly. The river was saved. Later, in 1927, the Olmos Dam was built to control flooding upstream; a bypass channel downtown was completed in 1930.

In 1929, architect Robert Hugman proposed a plan to beautify the river with walkways, landscaping, and shops that would attract visitors to the area. Influenced by his visits to the French Quarter in New Orleans, and its cultural attraction, his designs blended San Antonio's Hispanic cultural aesthetic with a hint of Venetian charm. Hugman's plans also proposed engineering aspects to further alleviate potential flooding. His vision was a good one, backed by the mayor, but it did not materialize due to construction plan disagreements, including doubts on the part of the Conservation Society.

Maury Maverick, Sr. served as U.S. congressman from the 20th District (1935–38), where he organized a group of "maverick" legislators who sponsored legislation to "out-New Deal" FDR's New Deal. His 1937 autobiography, *A Maverick American,* was something of a Depression-era bestseller. He was not only a political ally, but the stamp collecting friend of President Franklin Delano Roosevelt. He was able to influence a gift to San Antonio of $325,000 from the National Youth Administration to fund the River Beautification project. Maverick, along with then Mayor C. K. Quinn and hotel owner Jack White, devised a plan. To leverage the $400,000.00 needed for the project, they proposed a .015 tax and obtained the remaining $75,000. Finally, Robert Hugman's vision, though somewhat rearranged, was to be realized. The groundbreaking ceremony was in March of 1939. This, in itself is a story that has more interesting turns, including the arched bridges, and the colorful Arneson River Theater, with Rositas Bridge, and livelihood on the Riverwalk.

Maury Discovers the Village

Rivers have always been where civilizations begin, and here is another chapter about a little village, growing beside a river, yet striving to retain its character. Amidst all the San Antonio Riverwalk construction, one starry night, newly elected mayor, Maury Maverick, Sr. was walking along the river. He ambled up the bank to find the little village with, legend has it, a full Moon above, guiding him and lighting the way. What he saw in the luminous glow was a village with its adobe cottages, like some strange and innocent dusty anachronism. San Antonio's growing downtown and its 403-foot-tall Smith-Young Tower was nearby, along with other surrounding buildings. The city was growing and progressing—yet here was this place, lost in time.

The next day, Maverick returned. He found the area by daylight to be in a distressing condition. There were large piles of rubbish, old iron beds, abandoned cars and car parts, a cistern full of pots, pans, daggers, dirt, broken chairs, and more. The people living there were surviving in slum conditions, with no running water or electricity. Some cottages had only dirt floors and were crowded with up to four generations of family. How could this be a part of downtown San Antonio?

Terrellita, his daughter, recalled that he would come home and talk about this village he had found, but would not take her there, because, in her words, "There was an impetigo epidemic and Daddy just wouldn't let me go until everything was fixed up better." Maverick knew something had to be done to clean up this area, and hopefully to preserve the history and culture of this village. Later he would envision even more possibilities to carry out his plan of creating a historic arts village.

Maverick Decisions

Terrell Maverick Webb, Maury's widow, was interviewed in 1977, 23 years after Maury's death, by Brooke Allison in Austin, Texas, at her home. As I read that expressive interview, I can just hear her. I called her Nanny, because she was my grandmother, and such a character. Terrell said that if not for this project—this vision of Maury's—the area would have been leveled, for possibly another parking lot or bank building. The land was owned by the Public Works Company, so, what Maverick did was trade land with Public Works, and he was able to acquire La Villita for the City of San Antonio.

Before this could happen, though, something needed to be done to help the people who were living in such unhealthy conditions. Anyone aware of Maury Maverick, Sr.'s political career knows that he was keenly concerned about people living in poverty and was dedicated to solving their problems, often at his own political expense.

La Villita was hardly his first venture into this arena. In 1932 he had created a DIGA colony in San Antonio. As stated by Maverick, "DIGA [was] an anagram of letters out of Agricultural and Industrial Democracy."[1] This was an innovative creation of Maverick's to relieve the suffering of the poor, many of them war veterans, by housing them, training them and using their skills. During this time he also worked with Father Carmelo Tranchese to secure funds from the National Youth Administration (NYA) to create Alazan Apache Courts and four other public housing "courts" in San Antonio. They relocated people who were living in slum conditions, sometimes in *jacales* with no floors, running water, or electricity. As stated by Maverick's stenographer, Laska Fortessain, the 119 people at La Villita were relocated also.[2] Again, he was turning to FDR's New Deal and Works Progress Administration, under which the NYA was operated for socio-economic reform.

On a larger scale, these programs put 8.5 million people to work throughout the United States during The Great Depression.[3] Maury knew the administrator of the N.Y.A., Aubry Williams, since he had previously asked him for help in funding the adjacent Riverwalk. Maverick resourced the Works Progress Administration and NYA not only to fund the Riverwalk project, but also for the renovation of the fortress walls and preservation of the irrigation ditches—*acequias*—of all the San Antonio missions.[4] The process of preserving and transforming La Villita was to be another example of his resourcefulness.

The Villita Ordinance

On October 12, 1939, Maverick secured the adoption of the "Villita Ordinance" as the basis for the project's vision. Maverick addressed the City Commissioners and a council chamber packed full of interested citizens. Among those present were historians, scientists, archeologists, and artists. His Speech began as follows:

We present today the Villita Ordinance. I want the people of San Antonio to know that in presenting the Villita Ordinance, it is not merely a plan to fix up some old

place for citizens to get entertainment, but it is for the social, moral, cultural, physical and financial benefit of the people and for the progress of human beings living in San Antonio.

He went on to talk about how the streets of the Village would be named after Mexican patriots. Bolívar Hall would be named after Simón Bolívar, who fought for South American independence, and Juárez Plaza after Benito Juárez, President of the Republic of Mexico. He mused about the arts and crafts that would be made in this historic village and how they should be "useful and true in design, hand wrought, and not manufactured." Adding his facet of humor, he assured the audience that this ordinance, written by 15 people, was the only ordinance in the world not filled with "whereas's, and "heretofore's, and hereinbefore's."

The ordinance began: "La Villita is officially hereby recreated and by this ordinance recognized as a project of the corporation of San Antonio, and a part of the life of its people." The principles and objectives of the project included: "To preserve the accomplishments of the past and build for today and tomorrow; to restore and develop a comprehensive community center, for the life, liberty, and happiness of the local citizenry; to promote peace and understanding between the American nations; to preserve Spanish and Southwestern culture; and to foster arts and crafts." There were more ideals, ideas, and details and the signature page included Mayor Maverick, the artist Blanding Sloan, architect O'Neill Ford, project supervisors, the City Forester, the City Engineer, the Consul General of Mexico, and other personalities, involved and interested in what could unfold.

Funding the Project

After the creation and official presentation of the Villita Ordinance, the National Youth Administration branch of Roosevelt's Works Progress Administration funded $100,000 and the City of San Antonio, its share of $10,000. Wonderful things began to happen. Another resource that Maverick turned to was the Carnegie Foundation, because his favorite aunt, Ellen Maury Slayden, and her husband, James L. Slayden, were friends with the Carnegies. Because of their interest in libraries, Maverick influenced them to donate funds to build Bolívar Hall, now the two-story building in the center of La Villita. The Public Library's Villita Texana collection was housed on the first floor, and upstairs was a large area for meetings and other events. Years later, the San Antonio Conservation Society had a museum downstairs after the Texana collection was moved to the San Antonio Central Library.

Making It Happen

Contributing also to the vision and success of this Historic Village restoration was the San Antonio Conservation Society, who worked with Maverick to see that the changes taking place were done in accordance with their standards. The task of preserving history while renovating crumbling buildings was not an easy one and Mayor Maverick was challenged by their guidelines. In turn, he and his staff gratefully sought the knowledge and help from this group of dedicated and focused women.

The cleanup and renovation of the Village was an undertaking with multiple benefits: it immediately employed 110 youth from the NYA, preserved the unique history of an almost forgotten portion of the city, and prepared the area for an array of events. After cleaning, preserving and restoring the old houses and walkways, it was time to get creative. Among the extensive collection of Maverick papers that were donated to the Briscoe Center of American History at the University of Texas in Austin, I found letters to The NYA administrators from Maverick, negotiating a wide array of subjects, from funding the repair of broken windows at the historical Cos House, to requests for historically accurate building materials, to large projects to hire many youth who would be employed while learning. One letter was from NYA administrator, J. C. Kellan, states that artist Blanding Sloan would be sent to San Antonio and funded to work on the Villita project. Another letter from Maverick requests that artist George Biddle be sent to add his creativity the project.

National Youth Administration (NYA) workers form bricks for the plaza and walkways of La Villita, December 1939.

The Artists at Work

Once the buildings were ready, talented people were brought in to practice their arts and crafts and to teach young people. One aim of this was to teach Mexican American youth the arts of their forefathers. These included the making of pottery and ceramic tiles, copper and wroght iron work, as well as carpentry and finer wood work. Ceramic clay tiles were carved in bas relief with scenes depicting San Antonio history, colorfully glazed, and fired on site. These tiles are now arranged around The Cos House patio. They begin with a scene of the Coahuiltecan Indians meeting Cabeza de Vaca in 1536 and end with a scene of Maury Maverick, Sr. greeting Franklin D, Roosevelt in 1939 in front of the Alamo, which was inspired from a San Antonio newspaper photo. The Cos house is an important historical site from which battles were directed and where treaties were signed. It has been the scene of many celebratory events since its restoration.

There are also decorative, hand-crafted ceramic tiles around the fireplace in the Bolívar Hall conference room and in the back workroom of one of the cottage shops. They are interesting because many depict the actual craftspeople and artists, working at their various crafts during this formative time. Some of these tiles can be viewed at the little museum on Villita street, Building 15, along with other artifacts and historical photos of the Village.

The Textile Program: Grant Writing in Detail

An area of expertise that was developed was weaving on large wooden looms, part of the textile program, which a favorite for public observation. Among the Maverick papers we also find a report of research for the staffing of administrators, and teachers of arts and crafts for La Villita's various projected activities to be housed in the little cottages and buildings. In a letter dated February 7, 1940, to Mr. J. C. Kellan, State Administrator of the NYA, from Grete Franke, Associate Advisor of Textiles, much attention was paid to this, to convince them to supply funding. An example of the amount of concern to represent the arts is shown through a human resource analysis of 24 individuals who were talented in crafts such as weaving and woodwork. These people were either very experienced in their craft, or teachers, or both. They were from various locations in Texas, Alabama and Oklahoma. Franke also gave recommendations on which of these would be best to hire as supervisory, teaching and other positions. For weaving, the report went on to describe the specific types of materials to be used— less expensive yarns for training and then better quality for final products. Attention to detail and color was important, stressing the use of indigenous dyes (red cochineal from local cacti, for example) and yarns made from Texas cotton and wool. The items to be made—rugs, curtains, tablecloths, wall hangings, upholstery fabric—would eventually furnish the various cottages throughout La Villita. Some of the extra pieces would be donated to children's shelters. Equipment to be made, such as weaving looms, were to be constructed according to historical models.

In addition, the memo included a plan of the training process of youth to be taught and employed. At the beginning, they would learn technical terms and details on the materials and loom parts and their functions. They would each be assigned to a particular phase and later be rotated to see which phase of the work each youth could do best. Eventually the students would draw to scale plans for certain weaves. The colors to be used would fall into a general color scheme, as chosen by the architect. Importantly, the proposal also recommended a reference library on craft techniques and design. This extensive proposal concluded that, by hiring only the very best staff and implementing the learning and working program, La Villita could become a useful place to observe standards of design and craft.

Oralia Flores (left) and Stella Toscano, NYA students, work on hooked rug in new weaving building at La Villita, September 1940.

A Legacy of Glass

One of the first artist demonstration studios to open that initial year was that of glassworker Larry Williams. (My sister and I remember our visits in the 1950s and '60s to watch this phenomenal work being done right there in a tiny adobe cottage. I remember seeing the detailed networks of clear lacey ice, made with fire, while he formed the roof of a carousel, with a circle of graceful, strong horses underneath. One of Williams's famous carousels was recently donated to the Witte Museum, in San Antonio. I returned to this same studio with my own children years later, and Williams was still fascinating to watch.) Larry Williams continued to create his amazing menagerie for 59 years, until 1997, helping to establish a long tradition of artists and craftspeople working for the public to view.

Opening Day

La Villita was becoming well known far beyond the borders of Texas even before its official opening. Because of this—and because the principle of comradeship, perhaps even solidarity, were prevalent in Maverick's vision—an important gift was given to the city by the President of Mexico, Manuel Avila Camacho, on behalf of the Mexican people. A towering bronze statue of the Mexican patriot, Father Miguel Hidalgo, was sent to Mayor Maverick to place at La Villita. On opening day in September, 1941, the statue stood at its home on the stage at Juárez Plaza. Later, under another mayor, the statue was moved to Romano Plaza, and according to my grandmother, Terrell, (1977 interview) "he is now directing traffic."[5] Again, the statue was moved back to La Villita, and eventually across South Alamo Street to the Instituto Cultural de México, near La Villita.

With the dramatic Hidalgo statue at the front of the stage, opening day at La Villita was a legendary and festive gala. Both Maverick and Terrell

Mayor Maury Maverick (right) gives novelist Thomas Mann and his wife a tour of the La Villita restoration project, February 1940.

were there, along with Ron Darner, head of Parks and Recreation, and Bertha Almaguer, who directed the dancers. Almaguer also played the violin, piano, organ and sang with an outstanding voice. Her dance students performed on that day in their dazzling costumes, sewn from beautiful fabrics and sequins that she had found on trips to her home country of Mexico. In close affinity with the standards of the Villita vision, she believed that children should remember their childhood as being filled with learning wonderful things, like dancing, making lifelong friendships, and knowing about their culture.

More Entertainment

During this festive, formative time at La Villita, other crafts and entertainments included the creation of elaborate puppet shows. They took place at The Little Church on Villita Street. The marionette puppets were made there, also. The shows were the idea of Rose Bernard, from the City's Department of Parks and Recreation, whom Maverick had placed in charge. She hired seamstresses, artists, writers and actors to create the shows that were performed there. Because there were no stained glass windows in the Little Church—or money to get them—the artists drew intricate designs on brightly colored cellophane, pieced them together, and glued them to the plain windows, creating a transparent and crinkled effect.

One of the puppets represented Maury Maverick, himself, complete with a costume made from scraps of his personal clothing! While one person worked the strings, Maverick's voice was used to carry on his part in the story. According to Terrell Maverick, the shirt tail on the puppet was deliberately left untucked, because he, himself often looked like this by the end of a long work day. The puppet was given to her and eventually she gave it back to La Villita, to hang in their administrative office at Bolívar Hall. The Maverick marionette was the narrator that introduced the play about San Antonio history, beginning with early San Antonio's "chili queens" and all that surrounded them, in the daily life at downtown's Main Plaza.

Terrell Maverick Webb Remembers

There were many other contributors to the progression of changes that took place as La Villita was transformed, as recalled by Terrell Maverick Webb. There was Hamilton Magruder, director of La Villita, who lived in one of the cottages during the formative years, with his wife, a teacher. Architect O'Neil Ford was on hand to advise on matters of historical construction and design elements. Mary Green, Art Activity Director, and Harding Black ceramist and teacher, were members of the original "faculty."

Integral to beautifying the grounds of La Villita was Stuart King, a genius with horticulture, from A&M University. Maury found him and nicknamed him the City Forester. He worked at several places around San Antonio and Terrell Maverick remembers him transplanting young oak trees from Brackenridge Park to both City Hall and La Villita. He also oversaw the tropical plants and colorful flowers that enhanced the adobe and gingerbread cottages. Today, a walk through this place is an even more pleasant experience because of its flora, numerous birds and squirrels, living happily in the home of their own lineage.

During her interview, Terrell was asked what she saw as the main purpose of La Villita. She replied:

> To save it, just save it for the town and for the world, for posterity, if nothing else. But then, it was wonderful that it could be used to give work to some of the great artists and great architects and the people who ran those agencies during the Depression and the war. They were sent down there (San Antonio) by the national offices to train other people, and they were paid by the government for doing it. There was something going on in every house. Those poor blind people coming in there and weaving, was the most inspirational thing I ever saw in my life. Yes, it was![5b]

Other reasons Terrell stated as La Villita's goals were to encourage Western Hemispheric solidarity, to keep it from becoming a parking lot, and to "get it for the City." This way, she said, the City "could place it on a historical level with the Missions, and the Alamo."

At the end of her long interview, Terrell could not find the sheet music for a song, "In Old Villita," commissioned by the City. She played it by ear on her piano for the interviewer, Brooke Allison. She was a fine pianist. Recently, the ornate sheet music was located among the family papers. This song, with lyrics by Ruth Warren Munn and music and chorus by Jeannette Feigenbaum, was illustrated by Blanding Sloane. It is an excellent example of the truly cooperative creativity that characterized La Villita.

La Villita Historic Arts Village Today

Over the years, La Villita Historic Arts Village's relaxed sense of daily life, its "seclusion and poise," has remained sedate and calmly creative, consistently drawing tourists and locals alike to wander its charming pathways, shops and studios. Even so, La Villita hosts numerous multicultural activities and festivals, large and small, that take place throughout the year.

An interesting mix of personalities frequent La Villita. On any given day, one may hear the beautiful sounds of a talented guitarist playing Spanish guitar, see an artist creating outside their gallery, or glimpse a shop cat stretching in the sun next to its favorite objet d'art. At other times, larger musical performances and varied festivities take place in Maury Maverick Plaza. Adjacent to La Villita is the Arneson River Theatre, unique because the stage is situated across the river, while the audience watches from the La Villita side. The two are connected by the lovely arch of Rosita's Bridge. This bridge was named after the well-known San Antonio singer, Rosita Fernández.

Annual Celebrations

For decades, the most celebrated event at La Villita took place during San Antonio's annual Fiesta. Begun in 1937 by the Conservation Society as a "river festival" celebrating the city's Native American heritage and its early colonists and settlers, the event evolved into "A Night in Old San Antonio," more commonly known as NIOSA. Fiesta itself, celebrated throughout the city, includes street and river parades and many various activities. It began as a celebration of Texas independence from Mexico, though it celebrates many Mexican customs. NIOSA at La Villita grew to ecstatic proportions until very recently, when portions of it were relocated to a larger space across the street in HemisFair Park. This part of Fiesta features all sorts of fun, food and music. Colorful booths and stages reflect the various cultural and ethnic groups who founded and built the city. To describe NIOSA in a few words: food, drink, color, music, dancing, laughter, *cascarones*, and great big fabulous hats, each a work of art.

Some Personal Memories of NIOSA

My memory of my first fiesta, in 1954, is a colorful blend of fun and terror, due to the somewhat nerve wracking custom of children (and adults!) smashing *cascarones* (decorated egg shells filled with confetti) on each other's heads. Even more memorable, though, was my mother as a Conservation Society volunteer who decided to entertain in an unusual fashion. What better way to sell soft drinks than on a "Medicine Wagon," fashioned after the Old West practice of traveling around the country to sell remedies? The "medicine" was my favorite drink, Birely's Orange (my sister's was Dr. Pepper), both sold to the public as a "remedy" for thirst. And, if people were not thirsty, they certainly were attracted to the old green and yellow wooden wagon with giant wheels, because Mom, Terrellita, was the dancing Snake Charmer on the wagon. I remember the dark blue glittering dress she wore as she danced to the music and offered forth Geraldine, a black King Snake borrowed from the San Antonio Zoo. I was quite intrigued by this mysterious scene, but this strange event never happened again. Even in the small crowd, Geraldine was not enthused, and when we took her home she wrapped herself around the bathtub's claw foot and would not let go until the Zoo people came and coaxed her to go back with them. That was, apparently, the end her entertainment career.

Another interesting memory of NIOSA is of the hand painted *bolsas*, which are large paper bags with original paintings by local artists. One year, I felt I had struck gold when I found a particularly detailed scene of NIOSA. It depicted papel picado hangings, and various recognizable characters, dressed in colorful fiesta clothing. Here was the Pretzel Man (really an architect), and here the Bird Man (really Stuart King, Maury's "City Forester"). In the painting, he is carrying a bird cage to represent the bird vendors of Main Plaza in the days of the Chili Queens. Both of these characters were part of the history of La Villita's restoration. I knew the artwork on this bag was special, and it turned out to have been painted by the well-known artist, Caroline Shelton, who also painted the first Fiesta poster in 1983, two years before I found this treasure. I believe her work has influenced my own paintings, as well.

Other Traditions, New and Old

It seems as if much of Maverick's vision is being realized in the day-to-day life of La Villita. As a politician, Maury Maverick, Sr. worked hard for the people. La Villita was his most festive project, compared to the serious issues he tackled throughout his political career. The projects he undertook were unusual and courageous. One of his mottos was "Life, Liberty, and Groceries." So, it is no surprise, and a fitting coincidence, that The Little Church of La Villita still serves the homeless and hungry at its food pantry. Its Starving Artists Gallery features the art of 30 local artists. It is located right behind Bolívar Hall and Casa Manos Alegres. The Starving Artist Show, an annual event since 1962, is held in early April. The show not only benefits talented artists of all mediums and gives them an opportunity to show their work, part of the proceeds help to fund the Little Church of La Villita's food program.

Other cultural festivals include the Diwali Indian Festival of Lights, The Coffee Festival, The Chanukah On the River, the Harp and Shamrock Society's Irish Festival, the International Accordion Festival, the Soul Food Gospel Festival, and many more.

El Día de los Muertos, the traditional Mexican remembrance/celebration of the dead (November 2) has always been popular in San Antonio. For the last few years, La Villita has branded its celebrations as Muertosfest, which now lasts for several days. This flamboyant and dramatic happening honors the cultural ideals of the original Villita Ordinance, in that it brings across our border a view of Mexico's cultural practices in a "combination and compromise" of ancient Aztec and Catholic beliefs. Large altars dedicated to a particular person or memory, are created by area artists or family and friends of the deceased. Each one is assembled with a distinctive theme in mind, so each is unique. There is even a contest for the best altar! In addition, there are vendors selling a colorful array of items created for the occasion, music, demonstration workshops, music and dance performances, and theatrical processions with painted-face costumed characters, giant papier mache' *calacas* and *calaveras* (skeleton figures and skulls) like one sees in various processions in Mexico, winding through the little streets with spiritual blessings, perfumed by sage and copal, with dancing and drumming.

During my most recent visit to Muertosfest, I sat on the Villita side of the outdoor stepped theater, watchingh as the riverboats passed, adorned with colorful sides of elaborate metal papel picado designs. Across the river on the stage of the Arneson River Theater were 18-foot-tall, colorfully costumed "Cassandra" mannequins, illuminated from inside, created by a local pair of talented prolific artists. Maury Maverick, Sr. would be thrilled by this mixture of the past preserved and present creative growth.

A Quiet Continuity

Through the years at the Village, the art galleries, studios and demonstrations have remained remarkably true to Maury Maverick, Sr.'s original vision. The Copper Gallery—featuring hammered copper work from jewelry to large sized bowls—has been in operation for 60 years. Some of the small shops and studios have been passed from one generation of artists to the next. Long-time residents include the Village Gallery, selling pottery and other crafts; Scentchips, which makes candle chips in the shop; Angelita's, selling natural fiber clothing and sterling and beaded jewelry; and the Guadalajara Grill. At the Mexican import shop, Casa Manos Alegres, which features hand-painted Oaxacan figures and other Mexican imports, visitors can often view artists from Oaxaca demonstrating their crafts in front of the shop. Nearby on Villita street, the owner of Villita Stained Glass crafts her own fused glass beads and other stained glass items in the shop. Each of these art-filled shops have been run by several generations of the same family. Other unique shops include the Capistrano Soap Company, operated by a third- generation soap maker, and Equinox Gallery, which features hand-crafted jewelry and contemporary precious metal works.

La Villita Historic Arts Village, not surprisingly, has hosted over the years a number of cooperative galleries, run by and for local artists. The River Art Group is a co-op gallery featuring artwork by 300 local artists. A smaller co-op gallery is The Little Studio. Galleria II, in the old Dosch Rische House, operated for 35 years until 2015, serving two generations of artists. Local artists, including myself, sold and demonstrated their crafts there. It was quite a special feeling to sit in that old adobe building, painting, looking out across the peaceful Plaza National, and thinking, "Wow. Thank you, Grandpa Hi, for making this possible." My older sister, Fontaine, named Maury "Hi" when she was about two, simply because whenever she saw him she'd say "Hi!" And he would say "Hi!" back so cheerfully. When you visit La Villita, go see the bronze bust of Maury Maverick, Sr. at Alamo Street and Maverick Plaza, and say "Hi, Hi!"

Today La Villita is listed in the National Register of Historic Places. Sometimes tourists will meander up from the internationally acclaimed Paseo del Rio/Riverwalk and exclaim about what a lovely place they have "found." Others come to San Antonio specifically to spend a day exploring the shops and experiencing the variety of visual creative expression to be found there.

The gallery and shop owners, and the tenants, artists and craftspersons, all share the feeling that they are privileged to work in this special place, a well-preserved remnant of Old La Villita, Old San Antonio. Within this sustained past, creativity finds room to change and expand as time moves forward. When a space does open up for a new tenant, applications are judged on the basis of how well they will fit into this historic arts village and how their own gifts of craft and creativity will contribute to the community.

Notes

1. Maverick, Maury. *A Maverick American* (Covici Friede, 1932), chapter XXII.

2. "La Villita Renovation" An Interview with Laska Fortessain. Blog post, Institute of Texan Cultures Cultures.

3. American Experience, "W.P.A. Surviving the Dust Bowl." online

4. Audry Granneberg. "Maury Maverick's San Antonio, Survey Graphic," Vol.28, No.7, July, 1

5. Allison, Brooke. "An Interview with Terrell Maverick Webb" (at her home, in Austin, Texas, 1977).

Bibliography

Henderson, Richard. *Maury Maverick, A Political Biography,* (University of Texas Press, Austin, 1970).

Maverick, Maury. *A Maverick American* (Covici Friede, 1932).

The Briscoe Center for American History, Maury Maverick Papers, University of Texas, Austin, 1939-1942.

Maverick, Maury (with 15 other authors). "The Villita Ordinance," 1939. San Antonio Public Central Library, Texana Section.

Rybczyk, Mark, *San Antonio Uncovered* (Wordware Publishing, Plano, Texas, 1992).

And, from memories of Terrellita Maverick, Maury's daughter, and my sister Fontaine, Maury's first grandchild.

Dedication
of
In Old Villita

Inspired by the high ideal behind the restoration of La Villita, the ideal of friendship between all nations in general and between North and South America in particular; believing firmly that in these troublous times, when nation wars against nation, race against race, and creed against creed, we have more need than ever before for some symbol to remind us that in the past other peoples have found it possible to live peaceably with their neighbors, that men of all faiths, Jew, Catholic, and Protestant, lived together in amity, that people from all over the globe here met and became true neighbors; believing that La Villita answers this need for such symbol to friendship and tolerance and good-will, we, the undersigned, have written, as our small contribution to this cause, the song called "In Old Villita," which song we hereby dedicate to that great American, Mayor Maury Maverick, whose firm belief in and practice of the principles of friendship between all peoples is an inspiration in itself, and whose firm support of the La Villita project merits full recognition.

San Antonio, Texas, December 28, 1939.

Jeanette Feigenbaum

Russ W. Nunn

45

IN OLD VILLITA

Lyrics - Ruth Warren Munn   Music and Chorus - Jeanette Feigenbaum

1. 'Dobe huts with earthen floors, An age old water well
2. Ghosts from countries far away, Old Germany and France,
3. Moonlight on the patio, love's story told in song

Copyright - 1939 by Jeanette Feigenbaum and Ruth Warren Munn
All rights reserved - including public performance for profit.
San Antonio, Texas
Copyright Transferred 1940 - To City of San Antonio - Texas.

46

48

October 12, 1939

Honorable Aubrey Williams
National Youth Administrator
Washington, D. C.

Dear Mr. Williams:

Herewith the original of the Villita ordinance.

We spent about three weeks work on it and you will
see that it has not only a very well worked out state-
ment of plans but that it also has illustrations to
explain it.

I WANT THE PRESIDENT TO SIGN IT AS A PERSONAL FAVOR
TO ME. This is, of course, entirely outside any custom
and never has been done before, but nevertheless, I want
it done. I also want Mrs. Roosevelt to sign it, and from
an emotional viewpoint, I want her to sign it more than
the President. I want you to sign it and also Dave Williams.

I will send a wire to the President when I hear from
you that you have received the original ordinance and that
you and Dave Williams have signed it.

Please read this over because this is something of
which we are very proud and we want and DESERVE National
Recognition.

Sincerely yours,

Maury Maverick, Mayor

MM:2

31 Oct 39

Carnegie Foundation
522 Fifth Avenue
New York, N. Y.

Attention: Mr. Keppel

Dear Mr. Keppel:

Herewith are the drawings of the Bolivar
Building for which we hope to get a grant from
you.

I hope that it is possible to get a grant
for at least $15,000.00 at once and then we can
go ahead and get the project approved.

I will appreciate your letting me hear
from you as to how we are doing.

With best wishes, I am

Very truly yours,

Maury Maverick, Mayor

50

14 Dec 39

Honorable Jesse C. Kellam
State Administrator
National Youth Administration
Austin, Texas

Dear Sir:

George Biddle is one of the greatest artists in
the world and has a world wide reputation. He made
the murals in the Department of Justice Building in
Washington, and is known all over the world.

Yesterday I passed an ordinance appropriating
$300.00 if he would come to San Antonio, realizing
that it was more or less a sponsorship. If he could
get $10.00 a day, plus transportation, plus expenses,
I believe he would come down. Even then he would be
getting less than he ordinarily gets.

If he came here, he would come for the purpose
of making a "survey" or "report". He would in no way
interfere with the administration, and it will be
principally for advertising purposes.

I should appreciate it if you would make application
to Washington for him to come here, and I am sure they
will do it on their own budget and not on yours.

With best wishes, I am

Sincerely yours,

Maury Maverick, Mayor

About the Authors

Maury Maverick, Sr. (1895–1954), was born in San Antonio, the eleventh child of Albert Maverick and Jane Lewis Maury Maverick. Albert owned a real estate and Land Office in the downtown Maverick Building; Jane ran their Sunshine Ranch and was important in civic affairs. Maury's grandfather was a Texas Ranger, politician, businessman, and memoirist. Samuel Maverick, Jr.; his great grandfather, was a Yale-educated early Texas politician and land baron. Samuel Augustus Maverick fought in the 1835 Seige of Bexar and signed the Texas Declaration of Independence. When it comes to Texas lineage, the Mavericks are in a class by themselves.

Maury Maverick, Sr. graduated from college and law school at the University of Texas. He was commissioned as a First Lieutenant in the 28th Infantry, 1st Division, U.S. Army, and received a Silver Star for actions in the Battle of the Argonne. Maury served as U.S. congressman from the 20th District (1935–38), where he organized a group of "maverick" legislators who sponsored legislation to "out-New Deal" FDR's New Deal. His 1937 autobiography, *A Maverick American*, was something of a Depression-era bestseller. As the mayor of San Antonio (1939–41), he was long admired for his reform-minded administration. Among the many progressive acts in his life—which included securing W.P.A. funds for the initial development of the San Antonio Riverwalk—he was proudest of the restoration of La Villita, preserving the 200-year-old Spanish village as a modern city grew up around it.

Lynn Maverick Denzer is an artist, teacher, and writer. Growing up on Sunshine Ranch in San Antonio as a descendant of Sam A. Maverick and Maury Maverick enhanced her interest in a range of topics from the beauty of nature to the passion of politics. Lynn studied art at University of Texas in Austin and the College of Marin, and received a secondary teaching degree at the University of Texas in San Antonio in English. Upon retiring from public education, Lynn pursued her own art, exhibing in several galleries, including High Wire Art Gallery, Carver Cultural Center, Bijou Theater, Galleria II at La Villita, the Jingu House at the Japanese Tea Gardens, and the Starving Artist Gallery at La Villita. Lynn continues to teach watercolor and other art classes at Inspire Fine Art Center. She is also involved in creative activities at Celebration Circle and San Antonio Art League.

Wings Press was founded in 1975 by Joanie Whitebird and Joseph F. Lomax, both deceased, as "an informal association of artists and cultural mythologists dedicated to the preservation of the literature of the nation of Texas." Publisher, editor and designer since 1995, Bryce Milligan is honored to carry on and expand that mission to include the finest in American writing—meaning all of the Americas, without commercial considerations clouding the decision to publish or not to publish.

Wings Press intends to produce multicultural books, chapbooks, ebooks, recordings and broadsides that enlighten the human spirit and enliven the mind. Everyone ever associated with Wings has been or is a writer, and we believe that writing is a transformational art form capable of changing the world, primarily by allowing us to glimpse something of each other's souls. We believe that good writing is innovative, insightful, and interesting. But most of all it is honest. As Bob Dylan put it, "To live outside the law, you must be honest."

Likewise, Wings Press is committed to treating the planet itself as a partner. Thus the press uses as much recycled material as possible, from the paper on which the books are printed to the boxes in which they are shipped.

As Robert Dana wrote in *Against the Grain,* "Small press publishing is personal publishing. In essence, it's a matter of personal vision, personal taste and courage, and personal friendships." Welcome to our world.

Colophon

This first edition of *Old Villita and La Villita Continues,* by Maury Maverick, Sr., and Lynn Maverick Denzer, has been printed on 80 pound coated matte paper containing a percentage of recycled fiber. Titles have been set in Apple Chancery type, the text in Adobe Caslon type. This book was designed by Bryce Milligan.

Wings Press titles are distributed to the trade by the
Independent Publishers Group • www.ipgbook.com
Also available as an ebook.